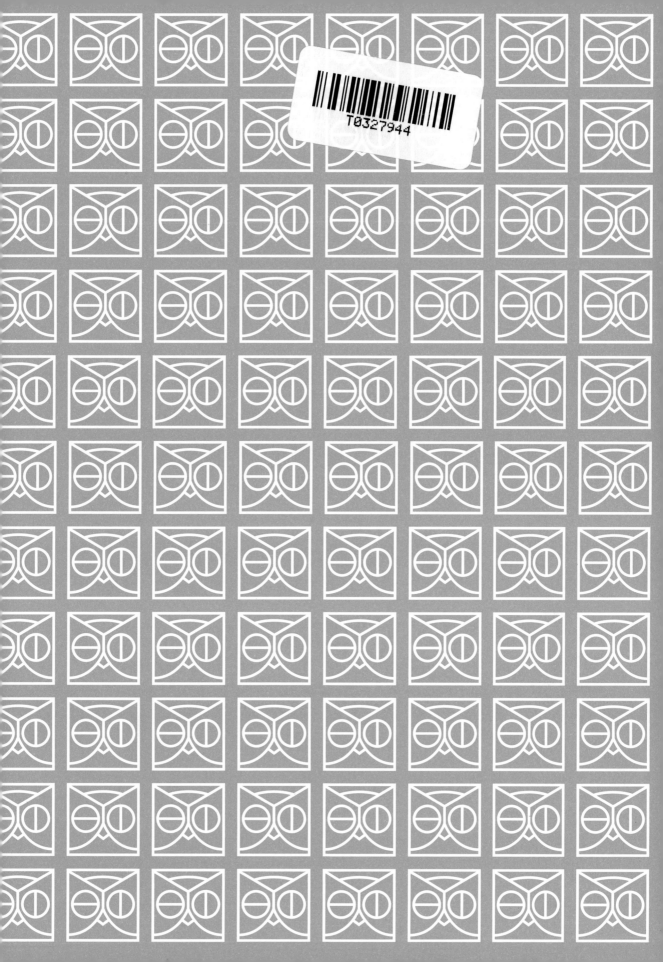

T0327944

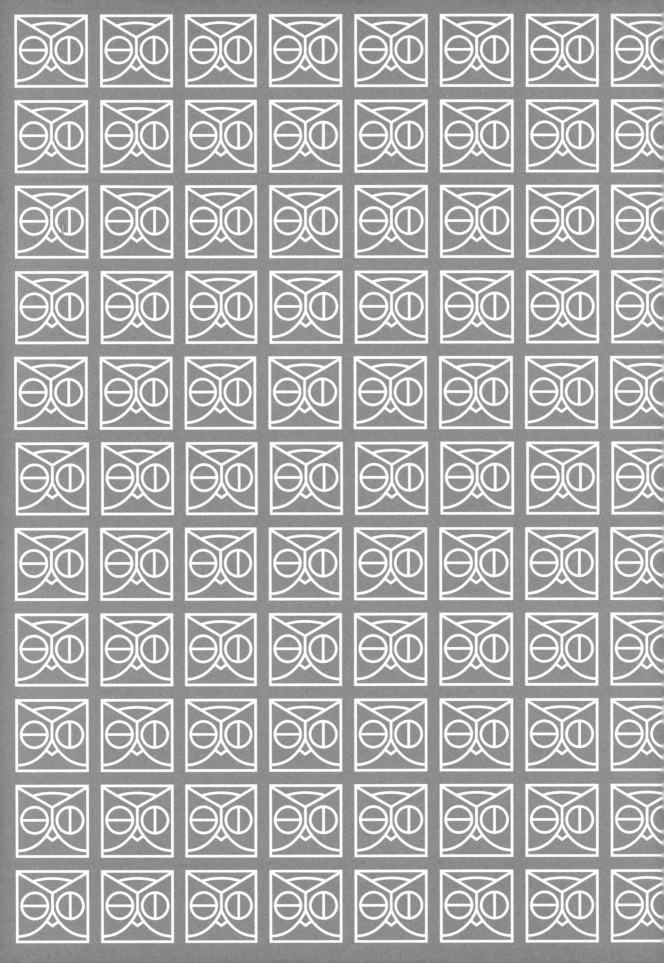

WILD&THEMOON

All photographs are by Greta Rybus, with the exception of those
on the following pages: pp. 5, 6, 16, 64, 67, 80, 97, 99, 100, 103, 110, 137, 138,
140–41, 143, 145, 146, 236–37, 241, and 252: © Sarah Arnould;
pp. 13, 29, and 248: © Juliet Dunne; pp. 182–83 and 230–31: © Eileen Cho

Book project proposed by Florent Massot
General Editor: Ariane Geffard
Editorial Director: Ryma Bouzid-Fuchs
Design: Delphine Delastre, for Flammarion
Food Styling: Océane Algaron
Recipe Formatting: Océane Richard

This book would not have been possible without the participation of Daniele Gerkens

English Edition
Editorial Director: Kate Mascaro
Editor: Helen Adedotun
Translated from the French by Tina Morrow
Copyediting: Wendy Sweetser
Typesetting: Claude-Olivier Four
Proofreading: Nicole Foster
Indexing: JMS/Chris Bell

Production: Christelle Lemonnier
Color Separation: IGS, L'Isle-d'Espagnac
Printed in Bosnia and Herzegovina by GPS Group

Simultaneously published in French as *Wild & the Moon:
Recettes vegan à base de plantes, de saison, sans gluten, délicieuses*
© Flammarion, S.A., Paris, 2020

English-language edition
© Flammarion, S.A., Paris, 2020

20 21 22   3 2 1
ISBN: 978-2-08-151338-9
Legal Deposit: 10/2020

Emma Sawko

Wild Recipes

Plant-Based

Organic

Gluten-Free

Delicious

Flammarion

"It seems to me that the natural world
is the greatest source of excitement;
the greatest source of visual beauty;
the greatest source of intellectual interest.
It is the greatest source of so much in life
that makes life worth living."

—Sir David Attenborough

contents

#introduction
living in harmony with yourself
by Emma Sawko

All around me, the city is throbbing, bursting with energy—sirens wailing, horns honking, funk music filling the air. An ordinary day in New York.

Leaning against a food truck in Brooklyn with my eyes closed, I bask in the sunshine as I bite into a delicious pizza. It's one of the best you can find here, and I savor the light, crisp crust and the well-rounded, tangy flavor of fresh tomatoes. I'm a native New Yorker, but I'm also a citizen of the world. Born to Parisian parents, I grew up in the Swiss Alps. I'm truly a child of my generation, one of those who've lived in several cities in the world, including Dubai, a place that sprang up out of the sand dunes. But first and foremost, I'm French—French in my passion for all that is fine, beautiful, and delicious.

That afternoon, I could well have been in the Middle East or in Paris. But it was there, in the Big Apple, that I began giving serious thought to this book. What would it contain? What would my message be? What recipes would I include? Who would I be writing for, and why? How would I tell my story in just a few pages? Above all, how would I recount the adventure of Wild & the Moon? I really wanted to get things moving along, to play a key role in the changes I felt were coming.

What if we could change the world with every meal we ate?

I finish off my pizza, thinking of what to include in my book. The recipes would be tasty, light, and vitamin-rich; food that comforts, is full of flavor and easy to make, food that respects our bodies and our planet. Recipes to make for yourself and for others, recipes to regale the guests and children sitting contentedly around your table. In short, the recipes that made Comptoir 102, my first concept store in Dubai, a success, and those that have become cult favorites at the Wild & the Moon juice bars. The book would necessarily include reflections on the state of our world, on the doors we can push open, the lines we can shift, the paths we should take, and the happiness that comes with imagining a different future.

I walk on, and passing another food truck—this one selling the very epitome of junk food—I smile as I think how the love of real food, sourced and cooked with care, is so closely intermingled within me with the food of my memories. What could better epitomize New York than its street food? What memories, and what inspiration. I want good food to be as accessible and as affordable as fast food. In other words, let veggies save the world!

Green is good and green foods rock!

A CHILD OF NATURE

A nomad I was born, a nomad I'll always be.

For as far back as I can remember, I've lived on the move. I was born on the banks of the Hudson, in New York, but three years later my family moved to Geneva, where I grew up beside Lake Leman, with mountains, bright skies, lakes, and meadows all around me. My parents chose to send me to an international school, where I was immersed in the rich environment of a multitude of religions, languages, colors, and cultures from around the world.

As a child, I dreamed of pointe shoes, of gliding and whirling through fouettés. One, two, three, entrechat! I took more and more ballet classes, admired Rudolf Nureyev, Jorge Donn in Ravel's *Boléro*, and Sergei Polunin, who are still my heroes today. My holy grail was to become a professional classical ballet dancer, and I even reached professional level.

In winter, we spent every weekend in the mountains, and even now I still feel they are my sanctuary. Mountain tops intoxicate me and I get drunk on oxygen, powder snow, and speed. If sport is the main pillar of my daily well-being, food follows close behind, and here I've been doubly lucky. My mother cooked divinely, and each meal was a time of shared joy. Always eager to learn new things, she became interested in nutrition very early on, understanding instinctively the link between food and good health.

My mother's core ethos was "health through diet," as advocated by Dr. Catherine Kousmine. She also drew inspiration from German naturopaths and soon turned to raw, organic food. Although we weren't vegetarian, we were already eating very little meat, and only meat from high-welfare animals. As for fruit and vegetables, they were on our plates at every meal, as were pulses and grains: there were lentils, chickpeas, flaxseed, buckwheat in abundance—so much, in fact, that my friends called our home the "seed house." My sister and I were raised on Budwig Cream, a combination of sprouted almonds, bananas, apples, virgin flaxseed oil, fresh fruit—a concoction that those same friends dubbed "gloubi-boulga," the favorite food of dinosaur Casimir, a character in a popular children's television program at that time.

In summer, we would leave Switzerland for the Basque region in France, where my parents' roots lay. Far from the beaches, from Biarritz and its surfers, we spent our time inland, near the little village of Saint-Jean-Pied-de-Port, surrounded by an expanse of green hills, where my great-uncle Batita had his farm. I can still smell the tomatoes we picked in the vegetable garden and taste the green beans and the eggplant fritters my great-aunt would make. Their wonderful flavors have stayed with me and have never been surpassed. There were also animals of all sorts: cows, sheep, chickens, pigs, and I'd live in symbiosis with them over the summer months, even insisting on sleeping in the hay with the newborns. Every year, when the month of August came to its inevitable end, I'd be heartbroken to leave, and today I realize just how fortunate I was to have had the opportunity to live so close to nature. Not everyone is lucky enough to become aware at such a young age of how important all things living are, of the inseparable link between the Earth and its inhabitants. Feeling the energy from beneath its surface, grasping the importance of living things, feeling the strength and force of the elements—all of these gifts have undoubtedly played a significant role in what I do today. The distance from "pitchfork to fork" isn't so great after all. And these enlightening experiences were as fundamental and irreversible as they were pleasant, joyful, and stimulating.

It goes without saying that during my teenage years I was a rebel, rejecting everything, cramming burgers, and abandoning ballet (still my greatest regret) and competitive skiing. It was a classic rebellion, a time when I wouldn't listen to anyone. However, what did prevail was the importance of cooking for me and a profound belief in respecting both food and my body. Today, this belief underlies all my habits: vegetables galore, whole cereals, nuts, healthy oils, light cooking, plenty of sport, and boundless respect for Mother Nature. My upbringing has caught up with me and branded me indelibly.

11 **introduction** by Emma Sawko

MY SINGLE GIRL YEARS

Who am I? Where am I going?

After a year studying at a hospitality management school in Switzerland, with little idea of what I was going to do, I landed a job in an advertising agency in Paris, with its big-city lights, bustling energy, and new people to meet. Soon, I was living life in the fast lane, working hard by day and going out every night with a bunch of friends, who soon became a second family to me. Every evening after work, we'd head out and party. I'd come home at dawn, exhausted but vibrant with life. After a reviving shower, I'd change and rush off to the office. I was hungry: hungry for life, for parties, for action, and for new experiences.

If you fly too close to the sun, you'll get scorched. The shock of my life came during this crazy time when I lost someone I thought of as my brother, my trusted confidant, and my soul mate, in a car accident. It took me years to recover from the grief. I realized I was not immortal, I had to slow down and take care of myself. To get back on track, I clung to my trusty life-jackets: sport and healthy food, the two solid foundations that had helped me get through my past excesses. My upbringing and the healthy lifestyle that had been inculcated in me prevented me from going off the rails. They acted as safeguards and showed me the way forward.

In my late twenties, I met the man who was to become my husband. He was working in banking and I was still in advertising. Into sports as much as I was, he was a man with a zest for life who loved friends and partying. We had a lot in common, including our values, and we soon had a baby daughter, Thaïs, whose arrival totally changed our lives. Thanks to her, at age thirty-two I was transformed, and it was the most beautiful of any of my experiences. I fell in love with motherhood. My transcendent love for Thaïs was overpowering and straight away it brought me a new awareness. What world had she been born into? What kind of planet would I leave her? For the first time, I was overcome with a feeling of responsibility and I realized that I aspired to a world of greater justice. These thoughts were barely nascent, so little was I aware of them, but I began asking myself how our planet's resources were managed, wondering about ecology, the sharing of opportunities, and people's actions and reactions to these topics. My mind was spinning. Shouldn't I change (everything)? Live differently? Take action? No matter, I did not slow down because, as Wonder Woman, I had to excel on all fronts. I was running to and fro between my baby, my job, my friends and social life. I was also a frequent flyer to New York where I oversaw large budgets. I was traveling at high speed—too high. At thirty-four, I was pregnant

again and then my world almost fell apart. My second life-changing blow. At six and a half months, I gave birth prematurely to Joseph. There was so much anxiety, sleepless nights, doubts, and tears, but then a true gift of life as Joseph was in good health. Sixteen years later, Joseph is a strapping teenager: sporty, competitive, charming, and funny, and he bears no traces of his traumatic birth.

But life had taught me a lesson and I decided to take it seriously. We can't spend our lives running: to catch a subway, a train, a plane, or to arrive in time for a meeting. It's simply an illusion to think we can control everything, unrealistic to think our bodies and minds are machines that our will can control. We have to press "pause" and learn to prioritize. In fact, I didn't have the choice and it was almost reluctantly that I was forced to slow down. In the words of Anna Gavalda, "life is stronger than you are," that's for sure.

After Joseph was born, I realized I needed to take time for us. I decided to work less so I could devote myself more to my children and my family. With hindsight, I understand just how right that decision was and how lucky I was to be able to make it. I had to call a halt to the whirlwind, take time to breathe; take time to get to know my children, to appreciate them and share their joys, both small and big. Time is a luxury and it's good to be able to take time to think, to reflect on one's needs and values, and answer questions that are just taking shape. When Vladimir, our third child, was born in 2006, I finally learned to slow down, to take care of my well-being, and at last find a genuine balance between my personal and professional fulfillment, as well as stability with family and friends. I'd made my choices and they were the right ones.

BITING INTO THE BIG APPLE

Early in 2006, my husband's company transferred him to New York. For a Franco-American, crossing the Atlantic meant the joy of returning to the city of my birth, the pulsating metropolis I love so much. It was with serenity that I agreed to stop working to follow my husband and settle back there, wondering what the city held in store for us as a family.

We didn't just like New York, we all fell in love with it. I quickly adapted to the rhythm of the city, starting my days with an hour of sport, then criss-crossing the city, visiting art galleries and museums; I was happy to get around much more than I had in Paris. In this whirlwind of energy, I began two activities that are now part of my routine: yoga and Thai boxing. Once out of the gym, I would go to juice bars where I discovered the pleasures of intensely green juices, packed with herbs and chlorophyll. At the time, freshly cut wheatgrass, that cleanses you and leaves you ready to conquer the world, was a new trend. It dawned on me just how powerful an effect a purely plant-based diet, where juices and raw foods were predominant, could have on my physical well-being, giving me greater awareness, more edge. On the East Coast and the West Coast, Americans were adopting the new wave of raw food, and I was initiated into veganisim, whose highly developed concepts I found inspiring. Juice bars were everywhere, I read widely, and the general environment was conducive to a finer understanding of the essential role that food plays in our health. In this prevailing atmosphere, I began cooking differently, gradually eliminating animal protein from my diet. I reflected more and more on our planet, our modes of consumption, my personal shopping habits, my impact on nature and the living habitat, as now I had the time and energy to devote to these issues, with no distractions. Little by little, ideas took root and grew, as did convictions and a feeling of personal responsibility. A desire for more far-reaching action began to take hold.

We had been in New York for three years and our children were thriving. I felt in sync with the city and sufficiently at ease to want to go back to work. A small voice inside me was whispering, "Create what you are missing." But what did I miss? A beautiful concept store for children—one that had all the brands I could only buy on my trips back to Paris. For a whole year, I worked on my project, fine-tuning it, getting the details right, listing the brands, making contacts, doing my market research, analyzing the competition, and imagining how I would decorate the interiors. When I found an attractive boutique, ideally located on Lexington and Third Avenue, everything seemed to be falling into place. Overjoyed, I was about to sign the lease when my husband announced we were leaving for Dubai. A meteorite falling at my feet could not have come as more of a shock. My project collapsed. What a kick in the teeth! I went from denial to anger to sadness. I was furious with fate and with life itself—I would have to leave New York and start over from scratch, far from the city I loved so much, where I had found a sense of balance and where I was about to launch my own business.

THE CHALLENGE OF DUBAI

February 2010. The first family visit to Dubai.

I hated everything about it—passionately, instinctively, viscerally. I hated the places, the atmosphere, the food, the sheer bling of it all. I wanted to run away, far from the endless miles of highways, the skyscrapers jutting out of the sand, and the chilly air-conditioned shopping malls with their rows of luxury boutiques. I was overwhelmed by a feeling of utter artificiality.

My days were spent visiting soulless mansions in gated communities. I searched desperately for a juice bar, a healthful restaurant, a boutique with some soul, or an art gallery. Dubai may appear to be the American dream on the shores of the Persian Gulf, but for me it was nothing short of a total nightmare. Nothing could be more superficial. I boarded the plane back to New York with my children, certain I could never be happy there. Spring passed and the kids finished their school year. My husband was flying back and forth between Dubai and New York and time dragged on. I had to resign myself to another move and reinvent my life. Again.

Children and baggage in tow, I landed in Dubai, determined one way or another to adapt the place to my needs and what I wanted, rather than adapt to it. The heat was torrid, the air humid, the wind full of sand. Fortunately, our trips to the sea and into the desert brought me some calm and the sunsets were breathtaking, but once the children were in school, I started wondering: How would I manage? What would I do? How would I survive?

"Create what you are missing." That same inner voice was whispering inside me again. This time the response was immediate: for as long as I can remember, I've always loved fashion and design. I'd create a haven selling all the things I love—somewhere that offered an alternative to high-end luxury and low-end cheap, the only options currently available locally. It would be my very own style, with, as ever, a touch of rock 'n' roll.

It would be a variation of what I'd planned for New York: a French-style concept store, for adults this time, selling all those cool, fashionable, stylish basics by brands not yet available in Dubai, with a café alongside. No question of conforming to local conventions and no mall location for me! I found a villa in one of the old quarters of the city, near the sea. And, of course, I wanted to be able to eat the kind of food I like: healthy, organic, mainly plant-based, and flavorful. All this in the capital of fast-food! Fundamentally, I'll never change.

The comments I had to put up with! "You'll *never* succeed." "A sugar-free menu with no soft drinks won't work here." "In the middle of the desert, nothing grows without chemical fertilizers." For months on end, I worked and reworked my ideas, countering prejudices, learning the rules of the country, finding allies, and tweaking my business plan. I signed contracts with my favorite brands. Gradually, my project was becoming a reality. The premises I found would be the perfect showcase for my "Comptoir 102," and I persuaded all those around me to put their trust in me.

But life brings nothing but surprises, and they're not always happy ones. My husband was suddenly called back to his company headquarters in Paris. My head was spinning, I was living the nightmare all over again. How should I react? Give up once again and return to Paris, with no plan or work? Or stay in this city, a city I still did not like but where I had a project? Prioritize our family or believe in my dreams? I was sleepless for weeks, tossing and turning through the night. My thoughts raced endlessly as I focused on this dilemma: follow my husband or stay alone with my three children? Stay. Leave. Try. Hang in there. Or not. It was torture. And then one morning, I woke up and my decision was made. I announced to my husband that this time, I would not be following him. I'd be staying in Dubai to pursue my dream: I'd be opening Comptoir 102.

The words of American author Marianne Williamson brought me inspiration:

> Our deepest fear is not that we are inadequate. Our deepest fear is that we are powerful beyond measure. It is our light, not our darkness that most frightens us. We ask ourselves, "Who am I to be brilliant, gorgeous, talented, fabulous?" Actually, who are you not to be?... Your playing small does not serve the world. There is nothing enlightened about shrinking so that other people won't feel insecure around you.... And as we let our own light shine, we unconsciously give other people permission to do the same. As we are liberated from our own fear, our presence automatically liberates others.
>
> Marianne Williamson, *A Return to Love:*
> *Reflections on the Principles of A Course in Miracles*

I was going to think of myself.

My dreams were important, too, and were worth fighting for. I felt very deeply that this time I had to put them before those of others, even though my own husband and children were directly concerned. I would dare to affirm myself fully, make a plea for equality of opportunity, true egalitarianism. I would not put up with condemnation and I would not condemn myself. I was going against customary behavior, against norms. I would not follow my husband for the moment, I'd seek fulfillment there in Dubai, and I was sure of my decision, braving the misgivings of others and the disapproval of many. It was *my* moment and the moment for Comptoir 102. I knew, as did everyone close to me, that nothing would stop me.

THE REVELATION OF COMPTOIR 102

And it worked!

This concept store stocked fashion brands that I love, designers I hold dear, jewelry both quirky and elegant, chic and bohemian objects, and all sorts of items guaranteed to delight. There was also a shaded terrace where customers could sip a homemade almond mylk smoothie, lunch on a seaweed-quinoa salad with cashew sauce, or enjoy a black sesame vegan ice cream—it was a little dining room to share with those I loved. My idea was that, with eight to ten tables, at least a few friends and my family might come to eat there, but I couldn't have been more wrong. The restaurant was packed, bringing a constant stream of customers to the boutique. Expats who hankered after healthy food and locals wanting to try something new were soon all addicted to the menu that was chalked on a large blackboard by hand and changed daily. Our menus were created around the produce delivered to us each day by an organic farm that had succeeded in growing fruit and vegetables in the sand, without the aid of chemicals but through their own tenacity and ingenuity. Plants at the farm were watered with a drip irrigation system, their chickens laid the most delicious eggs, and everything was tasty. Soon Comptoir 102 was full and I had to expand the restaurant. We received accolades and won several prizes, including best healthful restaurant in the region. It seemed unbelievable and my heart overflowed with joy.

Not far from there, I found a lovely house for my family. I remodeled it, redecorated it, and built an XXL kitchen. After school, the kids would arrive at Comptoir 102 on their scooters to keep me company. In the early morning, while it was still cool, I'd go jogging along the beach or take a yoga or boxing class. When I arrived there, the idea of pursuing a "chic yet green" project had seemed totally impossible, but I knew all along that it would be my life project. The life I was leading suited me because I had created it for myself. I had made the right choice and I was doing well again. I was breathing.

I quickly became aware of the growing interest in plant-based diets and that such healthy food could be tempting for people in other parts of the world. I was also thinking about my own situation as, even if my kids adored Dubai, I was missing Europe and was fully aware that we were living in a city where we didn't really belong. I could see the children growing up in an environment that was totally different from our culture. My husband was becoming tired of his trips between Paris and Dubai and I was missing him, just as I was missing Paris, my friends, and my family being together.

Gradually, I was coming to realize that we had to return to Europe. Not by giving up Comptoir 102, as that was unthinkable—I was far too attached to it—but I had to dream of something different. Once more, I had to create the environment I needed for my own fulfillment. I wanted to go back to Paris with a plan in mind and, furthermore, this time my husband wanted to launch a new enterprise with me. The moment had come to envisage something new that we could do together. We would promote the importance of a plant-based diet as being beneficial to our planet, and we could play a part, even if only a modest one, in helping the environment. In late 2015, I made my decision and left Dubai with my kids, ready for the next leap. I wanted to think big, to fully incorporate an ecological project into my upcoming plans. It would be clean, virtuous, constructive, and positive. I made a commitment to myself that I would not contribute to the widening of any gaps—the gap between what is benefical and detrimental to the planet, or to our health—but, on the contrary, try to bridge them. I am convinced that there is no better business than a business that does good. Wild & the Moon would be our contribution.

THE WILD & THE MOON ADVENTURE

Paris, where my heart lies.

Very quickly, the French capital felt like home again. I got together with my friends, my family, my group of girlfriends from way back, and was once more in the cultural swing of things. We returned to our apartment in the center of Paris, not far from the Tuileries Gardens, where I resumed my boxing training. The classic Hausmann-style façades, the zinc rooftops glistening in the rain, the café terraces, the vibrant culture—every detail was intoxicating, and I suddenly realized how much I'd missed it all.

We were kept busy, trying out ideas, few of which made the cut. We discussed the name; I wanted one that would be inviting and inspiring, offering the promise of new possibilities, of space, of surprises and dreams. We racked our brains. It would be a place where we could serve juices, of course, but as a Frenchwoman, it was also important to me to serve food that was healthy and, above all, *good*—no boring, tasteless organic dishes for me! After trying out every conceivable name, we settled on "Wild & the Moon." Not everyone was convinced by it, but I was and it carried the day.

Meanwhile, I was working on the menu. I devoured French and English cookbooks for ideas, endlessly trawled blogs, and drew on recipes from Comptoir 102; I tested countless versions of plant-based lattes, squeezed gallons of juices and prepared gallons of almond mylk, baked batch after batch of cookies, and experimented with soups, salads, and cashew nut cheeses. Our kitchen resembled a madman's laboratory until Sati, a talented Californian veggie chef, perfected my recipes. We had a new "seed house," just like the one where I grew up.

We were also on the lookout for the perfect premises, well located and in tune with our market and our target customers. I was carried along, carried away, consumed by the project, but I was happy and felt completely alive, despite doubts as to whether the French were ready for charcoal juices and ginger-pepper-turmeric shots.

Life went on. It was beautiful, intense. Our project was coming to life.

The first Wild & the Moon restaurant opened in February 2016, at 55 Rue Charlot in the Marais district of Paris, in the third arrondissement. Behind a modest façade with windows filled with hanging plants was a welcoming space, featuring industrial furniture, stripped walls, and all natural rather than synthetic materials (wood, glass, concrete). There was a large white bar where customers waited for their orders for smoothies, lattes, and other drinks to be made. At the entrance were fridges containing freshly prepared salads and bottles of juice and plant-based mylks, and ingredients were clearly displayed on our menus. The public flocked in, often sharing tables.

It was all beyond my wildest dreams. We proudly proclaimed our philosophy on posters around the restaurant: organic, plant-based, additive-free, gluten-free, cold pressed, unpasteurized, no plastic, and the healthiest, least processed, seasonal, and local ingredients. With the exception of "Marco Polo" products (those that don't grow in France, like avocados and cacao), we try to source

everything from small farms and, naturally, we use the best we can find. "Good for you, good for the planet, and delicious" is our motto.

One of my main concerns has been to get rid of plastic containers as I can't claim to be green if I add to the vast amount of plastic in the oceans. I'm kept up at night by the thought of the microplastics that are produced when debris breaks down, contaminating the seas and fish in them. When we launched Wild & the Moon, I was particularly concerned about this issue, which has taken the most time, perseverance, and greatest effort to overcome, but today we have managed to replace all plastic containers with a biodegradable plant-based material (cornstarch or sugar cane). It comes at a cost, but we're proud of it.

Naturally we must avoid food waste as well, so at Wild & the Moon we recycle everything by planning what we make ahead. For example, the almond pulp left over from making almond mylk is added to cracker and cookie dough. Our display cases are not overflowing with baked goods, as we prefer to run out rather than throw away any that are left over.

There is an expression coined by M.K. Fisher that I'm very fond of: "First we eat. Then we do everything else!" It's because everything else takes second place that I attach so much importance to the quality of what I eat and, naturally, what I serve to Wild & the Moon customers. I also believe in the benefits of superfoods. Spirulina, matcha, goji berries, maca, guarana, turmeric, and many others that help boost your energy, well-being, and health feature throughout the recipes in this book.

ACHIEVING BALANCE IN MY LIFE

Today, I divide my time between France and the Middle East, between our premises in Paris and in Dubai and Abu Dhabi. On a daily basis, my life is crazy, but I enjoy being "devoured" by Wild & the Moon, which is growing very fast indeed.

Despite all this, I ensure I maintain my balance by following a few simple rules:
– Every day I set aside one hour for a sports activity, generally in the morning, to rid myself of stress and feel in top form for the rest of the day.
– I make sure I spend time with my family and friends, often over a good meal. Eating well is one of my greatest pleasures, one I could not do without.
– No matter how busy I am, I make time for proper meals. In the morning, I prepare a banana smoothie with homemade almond mylk and some superfoods. I switch between a bowl of porridge with cacao and a chia pudding

with coconut milk and seasonal fruit. At our evening family meal we eat quinoa-spinach-vegan feta patties, chili sin carne, roasted vegetables with homemade hummus, or buckwheat balls with slow roasted tomatoes and a herb salad.

– From time to time I treat myself to something sweet such as an almond-orange blossom cookie, a square of raw chocolate, or stewed seasonal fruit with vanilla cashew nut custard.

– I make a point of devoting time to achieving inner calm, whether it be through a walk in the park on my way home from work, a few minutes of meditation or breathing exercises, a yoga session, or a hike in the mountains.

– I invest energy in friends by spending time with them, organizing parties, or taking vacations to Greece or the Basque coast with them. The shared laughter and joy boosts my energy and well-being, and the reserves of happiness I store stimulate me in the long term.

– I listen carefully to my emotions, my desires, my needs, and my impulses. I work on myself, accepting my ups and my downs, and I try to be my own best ally. I encourage myself, accept my limits, and, most importantly, I do not try to be perfect. Being compassionate with myself is a long-term project—an enormous challenge, as tough as it is liberating.

Wild & the Moon is not perfect. Many things still remain to be done and we are working on them continually, but the company is already making its mark with eleven addresses in three different cities: seven in Paris, three in Dubai, and one in Abu Dhabi.

I've often said that my dream was to make Wild & the Moon the organic answer to Starbucks. I hope one day we will have branches almost everywhere and our products will be truly accessible to all, so everyone can have the chance to eat healthily. Is this only a dream? Like the tale of the hummingbird who tirelessly brought drops of water in its beak to put out the forest fire, we are doing our part to work towards a change that is not only necessary and urgent but also the only one that can reconcile humankind with nature.

I hope I can accompany you through the pages of this book, guiding you towards a healthier lifestyle that is more respectful of nature, so you can find your own harmony. The object is not to attain perfection, or an ideal; it is simply to share tips for healthy eating through easy, delicious recipes, our little secrets for getting into shape, and the insights we've gained on this ongoing journey towards greater respect for ourselves and the planet.

Be wild!
#eatwise

#starters

. . . .

Starters set the scene. At Wild & the Moon, we like them colorful, light, plant-based, exotic, and bursting with flavor, mixing influences from near and far—from California to the Middle East. And the good news is that you can make XL portions of these starters to transform them into delicious main dishes.

konjac noodles with spirulina 28 **wild guac** 28 **hummus** 30 **avo toast** 33 **tomato beet** 35 **wild ceviche** 36 **pink hummus** 38 **creamy konjac noodles** 40 **wild muffins** 43

konjac noodles with spirulina

Serves 4

———

1 lb. (500 g) konjac (shirataki) noodles
2 tsp green spirulina powder
3½ oz. (100 g) vegan cream cheese (recipe p. 227)
Salt and pepper
To serve:
3 scallions, washed and finely chopped
1 tbsp (6 g) grated vegan Parmesan-style cheese

Thoroughly rinse the noodles and drain them. In a mixing bowl,
stir the spirulina into the vegan cream cheese, followed by the noodles.
Season with salt and pepper and divide between individual plates or bowls.
Serve the noodles cold, sprinkled with the chopped scallions and grated
vegan Parmesan-style cheese.

wild guac

Serves 4

———

4 avocados, halved and pitted
¼ onion, peeled and very finely chopped
½ garlic clove, peeled and very finely chopped
2 tbsp (30 ml) lemon juice
2 tbsp (30 ml) olive oil
Salt and pepper

Using a spoon, scoop out the avocado flesh into a bowl and crush it roughly
with a fork.
Stir in the onion and garlic, followed by the lemon juice and olive oil.
Season with salt and pepper. Mix well and adjust the seasoning if necessary.

hummus

Serves 4

¾ **cup (6 oz./160 g) dried chickpeas**
1 tbsp (15 ml) olive oil
1 tbsp (15 ml) lemon juice
1 tsp ground cumin
1 garlic clove, peeled and crushed
Salt
To serve:
Black sesame seeds
A few whole cooked chickpeas and toasted pumpkin seeds
Edible flowers, washed

1 Soak the chickpeas in a bowl of cold water for 12 hours or overnight. Drain and rinse well. Cook the chickpeas in a large saucepan of boiling, salted water until they are tender. Once the chickpeas are soft, drain, reserving ⅔ cup (150 ml) of the cooking liquid.

2 Reserve a few whole chickpeas for serving and put the rest in a food processor with the olive oil, lemon juice, a little of the reserved cooking liquid, cumin, and garlic. Season with salt and process until smooth and creamy, adding more of the cooking liquid as needed. Adjust the seasoning, if necessary.

3 Spoon the hummus into a serving bowl or onto individual plates. Scatter over the sesame seeds, reserved chickpeas, and toasted pumpkin seeds, and add a few edible flowers.

avo toast

Serves 4

---

5 oz. (150 g) plain gluten-free focaccia
2 tsp olive oil
2 tbsp (30 g) miso mayonnaise (recipe p. 224)
4 thin slices cucumber, the same length as the focaccia toasts
   (sliced lengthwise)
2 avocados, halved, pitted, and peeled
Salt
To serve:
1 tbsp (15 ml) pumpkin seed oil
1 tbsp (10 g) hemp seeds

1 Preheat the oven to 350°F (180°C/Gas mark 4). Cut the focaccia into 4 equal-sized rectangles. Place them on a baking sheet, drizzle with the olive oil, and bake in the oven for a few minutes until golden and crisp. Let cool to room temperature.

2 Spread the toasts with a thin layer of miso mayonnaise. Lay a cucumber slice on top and season lightly with salt.

3 Slice the avocado halves thinly, arrange over the cucumber, and season with salt. Drizzle the toasts with the pumpkin seed oil and sprinkle over the hemp seeds.

tomato beet

Serves 4

———

6 oz. (160 g) raw red beet, peeled and grated
½ garlic clove, peeled and finely chopped
1 small red onion, peeled and finely chopped
1 tbsp (15 ml) olive oil
2 tbsp plus 2 tsp (40 g) shiro miso
1 tbsp plus 1 tsp (20 ml) shoyu soy sauce
6 roma plum tomatoes (about 10 oz./280 g), washed and diced
To serve:
A few chive stems or scallion tops, washed and finely chopped
1 pinch fleur de sel
1 pinch sumac

 Put the beet, garlic, red onion, olive oil, miso, and shoyu in a bowl. Stir in the diced tomatoes until evenly combined.

 Serve with the chopped chives or scallion tops scattered over, and sprinkle with the fleur de sel and sumac.

wild ceviche

Serves 4

6 oz. (160 g) palm hearts, finely diced
2 small avocados, halved, pitted, and flesh diced
1 small mango, peeled and flesh diced
½ red bell pepper, washed, seeded, and diced
¼ red onion, peeled and diced
2 tsp olive oil
½ bunch cilantro leaves, washed and chopped
1 tbsp (15 ml) lime juice
Salt and pepper
To serve:
Blue poppy seeds
2 scallions, washed and finely chopped
4 lime wedges

 1 Put the diced palm hearts, avocados, mango, red bell pepper, and onion in a bowl. Add the olive oil, cilantro leaves, and lime juice. Season with salt and pepper and stir lightly to combine everything.

 2 Spoon into individual bowls and serve sprinkled with blue poppy seeds and the chopped scallions. Accompany with the lime wedges to squeeze over.

pink hummus

Serves 4

___

¾ cup (6 oz./160 g) dried chickpeas
1 tbsp (15 ml) olive oil
1 tbsp (15 ml) lemon juice
3 oz. (80 g) tahini
1 tbsp (15 ml) beet juice
Salt
To serve:
1 tsp black sesame seeds or
1 handful cooked chickpeas

1 Soak the chickpeas in a bowl of cold water for 12 hours or overnight. Rinse and drain well. Cook the chickpeas in a large saucepan of boiling, salted water for about 40 minutes until they are tender. Once soft, drain the chickpeas, reserving a small amount of the cooking liquid.

2 Place the chickpeas with a little of the reserved cooking liquid, olive oil, lemon juice, and tahini in a food processor and season with salt. Process until smooth and creamy, adding more of the cooking water liquid as needed. Adjust the seasoning, if necessary, and stir in the beet juice, mixing well.

3 Transfer the hummus to a serving bowl or individual dishes and scatter over black sesame seeds or cooked chickpeas, according to personal preference.

creamy konjac noodles

Serves 4

1 lb. (500 g) konjac (or kelp) noodles
1 carrot, peeled and grated or cut into julienne strips
1 scallion, washed and finely chopped
A few cilantro leaves, washed and finely chopped
3½ oz. (100 g) white cashew sauce (recipe p. 224)
1 small pinch Cayenne pepper
Salt
To serve:
Fresh red chili slices
A few drops lime juice
A few cilantro leaves, washed and finely chopped
1 small handful peanuts, toasted

1 Soak the noodles in a bowl of cold water in the refrigerator while you prepare the other ingredients.

2 Thoroughly drain the noodles and mix with the carrot, scallion, cilantro, and white cashew sauce. Season with the Cayenne pepper and salt. Mix everything together carefully.

3 Divide between individual plates. Serve topped with red chili slices, drizzled with the lime juice, and sprinkled with chopped cilantro and toasted peanuts.

wild muffins

Makes 10

5 oz. (150 g) sweet potato, peeled and diced
1⅓ cups (7 oz./200 g) rice flour
1½ cups (5 oz./150 g) gluten-free rolled oats
2 oz. (60 g) chia seeds
1 oz. (30 g) sunflower seeds
1 tbsp (10 g) gluten-free baking powder
1 pinch salt
Scant ½ cup (100 ml) olive oil, plus a little extra
  for coating the sweet potato
Generous ¼ cup (2½ oz./70 g) French mustard
1½ cups (340 ml) almond mylk (recipe p. 218)
3½ oz. (100 g) spinach leaves, washed and finely shredded
1 carrot, peeled and grated
1 cup (6 oz./160 g) cooked chickpeas
2 tbsp poppy seeds

 Preheat the oven to 425°F (220°C/Gas mark 7). Line 10 cups of a muffin pan with paper muffin cases or parchment paper. Toss the diced sweet potato in a little olive oil until coated, spread out on a baking sheet lined with parchment paper, and bake for 15–20 minutes until tender but not browned.

 Meanwhile, mix together the rice flour, rolled oats, chia seeds, sunflower seeds, baking powder, and salt. Gradually stir in the olive oil, followed by the mustard, and then the almond mylk. Stir in the spinach and carrot, followed by the chickpeas and diced sweet potato. Reduce the oven temperature to 325°F (160°C/Gas mark 3).

 Divide the batter among the muffin cups and sprinkle with the poppy seeds. Bake for 35 minutes, until well risen and a cake tester inserted into one of the muffins comes out clean. Cool on a wire rack. Serve warm or cold.

#soups

....

Whether it's winter or summer, there's always
hot or chilled soup on our menu. Soups are
the perfect comfort food, as they satisfy your
appetite and give your health a boost.
The ultimate Wild & the Moon tip: combine fruit
and vegetables, as we do in some of our
recipes, to put a spring in your step.

abuela's

Serves 4

½ cup (3½ oz./100 g) dried chickpeas
4 cups (1 liter) water
1 onion, peeled and chopped
1 garlic clove, peeled and chopped
3 tbsp (45 ml) olive oil
1 tsp ground cumin
1 tsp paprika
1 tsp Cayenne pepper
1 sprig rosemary, washed
1 sprig thyme, washed
1 bay leaf, washed

5–6 small tomatoes, washed and diced
1 carrot with its green top, peeled
 and diced
1 celery stalk, washed and diced
1–2 medium-sized zucchini
 (total weight 7 oz./200 g),
 washed and diced
Juice of 1 lemon
Salt
To serve:
Fresh herbs
Sumac

 Soak the chickpeas in a bowl of cold water for 12 hours or overnight. Drain and rinse well. Pour the 4 cups (1 liter) water into a large saucepan, add the chickpeas, and season with salt. Bring to a boil and cook until the chickpeas are tender. Once the chickpeas are soft, blend two-thirds of them with a little of the cooking liquid. Reserve the rest of the cooking liquid, as well as the remaining one-third of the chickpeas (for serving).

 Cook the onion and garlic in a little of the olive oil in a large saucepan over low heat, until softened but not colored. Stir in the spices and herbs and cook for 1–2 minutes, until lightly golden. Add the diced vegetables with the rest of the olive oil and fry for a few minutes. Add the lemon juice, blended chickpeas, and the remaining cooking liquid, and season with salt. Cover and cook over low heat until all the vegetables are tender.

 Remove and discard the bay leaf. Add the reserved cooked chickpeas and stir them in carefully so as not to crush them. Serve the soup hot, sprinkled with chopped fresh herbs and sumac.

mamatita

Serves 4

---

1 small onion, peeled and chopped
1 garlic clove, peeled and chopped
1 tbsp (15 ml) olive oil
1 tsp caraway seeds
1 sprig fresh rosemary, washed
1 sprig fresh thyme, washed
2 bay leaves, washed
1 large carrot, peeled and diced
1 celery stalk, washed and chopped
3½ cups (800 ml) water
Scant ½ cup (3½ oz./100 g) green split peas
½ cup (2 oz./50 g) chickpeas, cooked
4 tbsp (60 g) basil pesto (recipe p. 227)
1 tsp tamari
Salt and pepper

 Cook the onion and garlic in the olive oil in a large saucepan over low heat, until softened but not colored. Add the caraway seeds and herbs and cook for 1–2 minutes, or until the onion is golden.

 Add the carrot and celery to the onion and garlic and fry for a few minutes. Pour in the water, add the split peas, and bring to a boil.
Season with salt and pepper. Leave to cook over low heat for 20–30 minutes, stirring occasionally.

 Once the vegetables are tender, add the chickpeas. Remove and discard the bay leaves and ladle the soup into serving bowls. Accompany each bowl with a spoonful of basil pesto and a drizzle of tamari.

pumpkin

Serves 4

1 white onion, peeled and chopped
1 garlic clove, peeled and chopped
½-in. (1-cm) piece fresh ginger, peeled and finely chopped
3 tbsp (45 ml) olive oil
½ sprig fresh rosemary, washed and finely chopped
1 Hokkaido pumpkin, peeled, seeds and fibers removed
2 large carrots, peeled and diced
3 cups (700 ml) water
⅓ cup (80 ml) coconut milk
Salt and pepper
To serve:
Poppy seeds and/or black sesame seeds

1 Cook the onion, garlic, and ginger in a little of the olive oil in a large saucepan over low heat, until softened but not colored.
Add the rosemary and cook for 1–2 minutes.

2 Dice the pumpkin flesh, add to the saucepan with the carrots, and cook until golden. Season with salt and pepper.

3 Pour in the water, simmer until the pumpkin is cooked, and then blend. Add the coconut milk and blend again to make a smooth, creamy soup. Serve the soup hot in bowls, sprinkle with poppy seeds and/or sesame seeds, and drizzle with the remaining olive oil.

king kale

Serves 4

———

1 small yellow onion, peeled and chopped
1 garlic clove, peeled and chopped
1 tbsp (15 ml) olive oil
1 medium-sized head broccoli (about 14 oz./400 g),
  washed and chopped
About 10 kale leaves, washed and shredded
3¾ cups (880 ml) water
⅓ cup (80 ml) coconut milk
Salt and pepper
To serve:
Green scallion tops, washed and very finely chopped
Edible flowers, washed

1 Cook the onion and garlic in half the olive oil in a large saucepan over low heat, until softened but not colored. Increase the heat to medium-high and cook for 1–2 minutes, until the onion is golden.

2 Add the broccoli and kale to the saucepan with the rest of the olive oil, season with salt and pepper, and cook for a couple of minutes.

3 Pour in the water, bring to a boil, and simmer until the vegetables are tender. Add the coconut milk and blend everything together to make a smooth, creamy soup. Serve the soup hot, topped with chopped scallion tops and edible flowers.

cauliflower & coconut

Serves 4

----

1 small onion, peeled and chopped
1 small garlic clove, peeled and chopped
3 tbsp (45 ml) olive oil
½-in. (1-cm) piece fresh ginger, peeled and grated
1 small cauliflower, washed and chopped
1⅔ cups (400 ml) water
⅓ cup (80 ml) coconut milk
Salt and pepper
To serve:
1½ tsp gomasio
3½ tbsp (20 g) cedar pine nuts

1 Cook the onion and garlic in a little of the olive oil in a large saucepan over low heat, until the onion is translucent. Add the ginger and cook for 1–2 minutes, until golden.

2 Add the cauliflower and remaining olive oil and cook until lightly colored.

3 Pour in the water, bring to a boil, and season with salt and pepper. Lower the heat and simmer gently until the cauliflower is cooked. Blend with the coconut milk to make a smooth, creamy soup. Serve the soup hot in bowls, sprinkled with the gomasio and cedar nuts.

miso shitake

Serves 4

1 tbsp (15 g) ground wakame
4 cups (1 liter) water
1 onion, peeled and chopped
1 garlic clove, peeled and chopped
2 tbsp (30 ml) toasted sesame oil
11 oz. (300 g) button mushrooms, washed and sliced
7 oz. (200 g) shitake mushrooms, washed and sliced
A drizzle of tamari
1 oz. (25 g) miso paste
1 pinch Cayenne pepper
2 handfuls spinach leaves, washed and shredded
½ bunch flat-leaf parsley, washed and chopped
Salt and pepper

 Dilute the wakame in about 4 cups (1 liter) water. Cook the onion and garlic in a little of the sesame oil in a large saucepan over low heat, until softened but not colored.

 Add the mushrooms and a little more of the oil and cook for a few minutes. Deglaze with the tamari and pour in the wakame water. Add the miso paste, reduce the heat to low, and simmer gently for 20–30 minutes.

 Add the Cayenne pepper and remaining sesame oil, and season with salt and pepper. Stir in the spinach and parsley and cook for a further 2 minutes before serving.

pineapple & cucumber

Serves 4

---

1 cucumber, peeled and cut into chunks
1 pineapple, peeled, and flesh cut into chunks
2 small scallions, washed and chopped
⅓ cup (80 ml) water
1 tbsp (15 ml) olive oil
A dash of lemon juice
3 oz. (80 g) macadamia nuts, toasted and roughly chopped
Several sprigs cilantro, washed
Salt
To serve:
Toasted macadamia nuts
Finely chopped scallion

 Process or blend the cucumber and pineapple with the scallions and water. Add the olive oil, lemon juice, macadamia nuts, and cilantro. Process again to make a soup with a thick, coarse consistency. Season with the salt.

 Serve the soup well chilled, garnished with toasted macadamia nuts and finely chopped scallion.

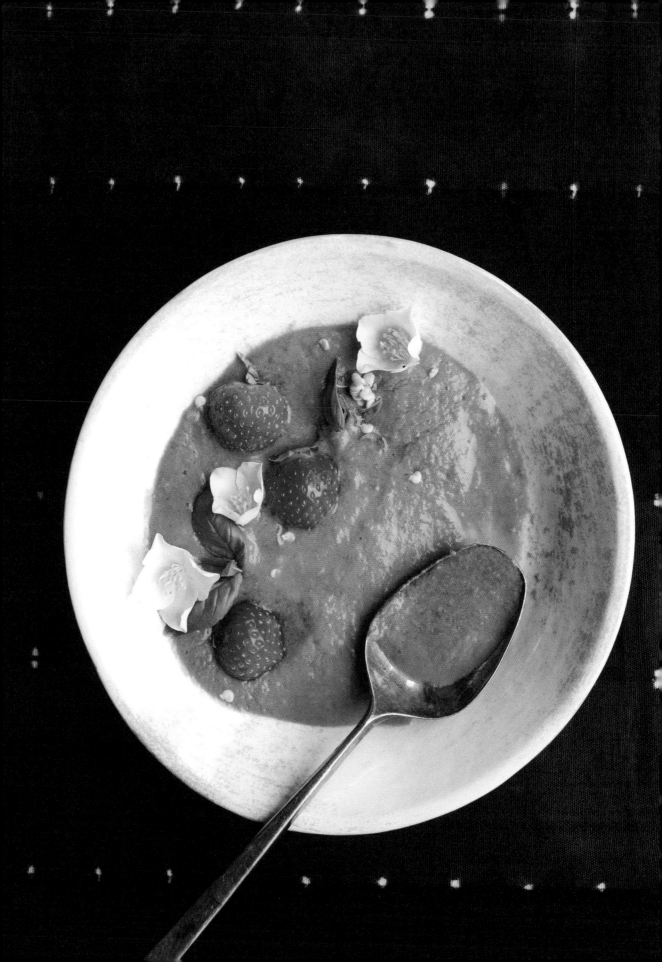

strawberry gazpacho

Serves 4

6 large very ripe tomatoes, washed and cut into chunks
1 large red bell pepper, washed, seeded, and cut into chunks
½ cucumber, washed and cut into chunks
½ fennel bulb, washed and chopped
1 small celery stalk, washed and chopped
1 small red onion, peeled and finely chopped
1 garlic clove, peeled and finely chopped
Small sprig fresh thyme, washed
1 pinch chili powder
2 tbsp (30 ml) cider vinegar
6 strawberries, washed and chopped
Salt
To serve:
A few basil leaves, washed
A few strawberries, washed
Edible flowers, washed

 Process the vegetables, garlic, thyme leaves, chili, vinegar, and strawberries together until smooth, adding a little water if necessary, as the soup should not be too thick. Season with salt.

 Serve in individual bowls topped with basil leaves, strawberries, and edible flowers.

#daily specials

· ·

"Eating just vegetables won't fill you up." "Vegan
dishes are tasteless." "Where will you get your protein
from, if not from animals?" When it comes to plant-based
dishes, the clichés are endless.

With a little creativity, experimenting with textures
and tastes, using spices and fresh herbs generously,
and adding garnishes, you can transform your meals.
What's more, these days you don't have to serve
dinner guests a fish or meat main course.
For true cool, choose 100 percent plant-based dishes.

the great polenta

Serves 4

———

1 garlic clove, peeled and finely chopped
1 small onion, peeled and finely chopped
4 tbsp (60 ml) olive oil
⅔ cup (160 ml) coconut milk
3¼ cups (800 ml) almond mylk (recipe p. 218)
1 cup (5 oz./140 g) polenta
A few sage leaves, washed and finely chopped
4½ oz. (120 g) vegan Parmesan-style cheese, grated
3 or 4 red-skinned radishes, washed
1 small sweet potato, peeled
1 small beet, washed
2 oz. (60 g) fresh peas
Salt and pepper
To serve:
Sunflower seeds
Pumpkin seeds

1 Briefly fry the garlic and onion in a little of the olive oil in a large saucepan over medium heat. Deglaze with the coconut milk and almond mylk and bring to a boil. Add the polenta in a steady stream, stirring constantly, followed by the sage, and let cook over medium heat until the polenta comes away from the sides of the saucepan. Add the vegan Parmesan-style cheese, season with salt and pepper, and remove from the heat.

2 Using a mandolin or sharp knife, cut the radishes, sweet potato, and beet into thin slices. Add the peas to a saucepan of boiling, salted water, cook for a few seconds, and then drain. Mix the sliced vegetables, peas, and remaining olive oil together in a bowl, and season with salt and pepper.

3 Serve the polenta topped with the vegetable salad and sprinkled with sunflower and pumpkin seeds.

walnut pita sandwich

Serves 4

Scant 2 cups (7 oz./200 g) walnuts
4 whole wheat pita breads
1 tomato, washed and thinly sliced
1 cucumber, washed and thinly sliced
1 avocado, peeled, pitted, and flesh thinly sliced
1 small scallion, washed and sliced
For the tahini sauce:
1 tbsp (15 ml) tahini
A generous drizzle of olive oil
2 tbsp (30 ml) water
Juice of 1 lemon
1 pinch garlic powder
Salt and pepper
To serve:
Arugula
Citrus vinaigrette (recipe p. 223)
Pine nuts

 Soak the walnuts in a bowl of cold water overnight. Drain and roughly chop them. Cut the pita breads in half crosswise and carefully open up each half to make a pocket. Set aside with the walnuts and the prepared vegetables while you make the tahini sauce.

 Combine all the tahini sauce ingredients together in a mixing bowl. Season with salt and pepper to taste.

 To assemble the pita sandwiches, divide the tomato and cucumber slices between the pita bread pockets and arrange the avocado slices and chopped walnuts on top. Spoon over the tahini sauce and scatter with the sliced scallion. Serve the sandwiches with the arugula dressed with the citrus vinaigrette and sprinkled with pine nuts.

Note: Soaking the walnuts overnight helps them absorb the tahini sauce better.

wild dhal

Serves 4

4 tbsp (60 ml) olive oil
2 small eggplants, washed and cut
  into large chunks
1 small cauliflower, washed and cut
  into large florets
2 large onions, peeled and chopped
1 large garlic clove, peeled and
  chopped
½-in. (1-cm) piece fresh ginger,
  peeled and finely chopped
1 small celery stalk, washed
  and chopped
1 tsp cardamom seeds
1 tsp ground turmeric

½ tsp paprika
1 tsp caraway seeds
1 tsp mustard seeds
1¾ cups (12 oz./350 g) red lentils
4 cups (1 liter) water
A few kale leaves, washed and finely
  shredded
Generous ¾ cup (200 ml) coconut milk
Salt and pepper
To serve:
Lime wedges
A few flat-leaf parsley and cilantro
  leaves, washed

1 Preheat the oven to 350°F (180°C/Gas mark 4). In a mixing bowl, season 2 tbsp (30 ml) of the olive oil with salt and pepper, add the eggplants and cauliflower, and stir until the vegetables are coated with the oil. Spread them out on a baking sheet and roast in the oven for about 30 minutes, or until the vegetables are tender and golden brown.

2 Fry the onions, garlic, ginger, and celery in the remaining oil in a large saucepan over low-medium heat, until softened, stirring regularly. Stir in the spices and fry for 1 minute. Add the lentils, stir well, pour in the water, and bring to a boil.

3 Simmer gently for 20 minutes, add the kale, and stir in the coconut milk. Add the roasted eggplant and cauliflower to the saucepan (or, if you prefer, you can serve the roasted vegetables separately) and continue cooking until the lentils are tender. Serve garnished with parsley and cilantro leaves and accompany with lime wedges to squeeze over.

japanese bowl

Serves 4

1 lemongrass stalk, washed and very
  thinly sliced
1 tbsp (15 g) miso paste
2 cups (500 ml) water
3 tbsp (45 ml) olive oil
1 small onion, peeled and chopped
1 garlic clove, peeled and chopped
½ celery stalk, washed and chopped
1 large eggplant, washed and cut
  into bite-sized pieces
1 small black radish, peeled
  and chopped
1½ oz. (40 g) lotus root, peeled
  and chopped
6 oz. (180 g) shitake mushrooms,
  washed and chopped
1 tsp ground turmeric

1 tbsp (15 ml) tamari
½ Hokkaido pumpkin, peeled,
  seeds and fibers removed
1 tbsp (15 ml) toasted sesame oil
3½ oz. (100 g) bok choy or Swiss chard,
  washed and cut into bite-sized pieces
1 green-skinned apple, washed, cored,
  and chopped
2 cups (14 oz./400 g) round rice
1 star anise
2 tbsp plus 2 tsp (40 ml) rice vinegar
1 tsp black sesame seeds
Salt and pepper
To serve:
A few flat-leaf parsley and cilantro
  leaves, washed and chopped
2 tsp sesame seeds

 1 Prepare a broth with the lemongrass, miso paste, and water. Preheat the oven to 350°F (180°C/Gas mark 4).

 2 Heat the olive oil in a large saucepan and sweat the onion, garlic, and celery over low heat for a few minutes without coloring. Increase the heat to high and add all the prepared vegetables, except the pumpkin and bok choy or Swiss chard. Sear the vegetables for 2–3 minutes, pour in the broth, add the turmeric and tamari, and season with salt and pepper. Bring to a boil and then reduce the heat to low. While the vegetables in the saucepan are simmering gently, cut the pumpkin into cubes and drizzle with the sesame oil. Spread the cubes out on a baking sheet and roast in the oven for about 30 minutes or until tender. Add the bok choy or Swiss chard, roasted pumpkin, and apple to the saucepan and continue to simmer gently until the vegetables are tender, and the cooking liquid has reduced.

 3 Cook the rice according to the package instructions in a large saucepan of salted water with the star anise. Drain, remove the star anise, and season the cooked rice with the rice vinegar mixed with the black sesame seeds. Divide the rice between 4 plates and spoon the vegetables and apple alongside. Scatter over the parsley, cilantro, and sesame seeds.

thai curry

Serves 4

---

2 carrots, peeled
1 large sweet potato, peeled
1 large yellow or red bell pepper,
   stalk removed and seeded
1 large slice Hokkaido pumpkin,
   peeled, seeds and fibers removed
1 tbsp (12.5 g) coconut oil
1 small onion, peeled and chopped
1 garlic clove, peeled and chopped
1 small celery stalk, washed, peeled,
   and chopped
½-in. (1-cm) piece fresh ginger,
   peeled and finely chopped
1 tsp curry powder
1 tsp mild chili powder
1¾ cups (400 ml) water

1 lemongrass stalk, washed and finely
   chopped
1 tsp ground cinnamon
1 tsp paprika
1 handful Thai basil leaves
1⅔ cups (12 oz./340 g) Thai
   jasmine rice
1¼ cups (300 ml) coconut milk
Juice of 1 lemon
Salt and pepper
To serve:
A few flat-leaf parsley and cilantro
   leaves, washed and chopped, or
A few cashews, toasted, or
A few pumpkin seeds, toasted

 Cut the carrots, sweet potato, bell pepper, and pumpkin into even-sized chunks.

 Heat the coconut oil in a large saucepan over medium heat and sweat the onion, garlic, carrots, sweet potato, bell pepper, pumpkin, celery, and ginger until the onion is translucent, stirring frequently. Stir in the curry and chili powders, season with salt and pepper, and cook for a few more minutes, stirring regularly.

 When the spices are evenly mixed in, add the water, lemongrass, cinnamon, and paprika. Stir in half the basil leaves and let simmer for about 20 minutes. While the curry is simmering, cook the rice in a large saucepan of boiling, salted water for 10 minutes. Once the vegetables in the curry are cooked, pour in the coconut milk, season with the lemon juice, and add the remaining basil leaves. Drain the cooked rice and serve with the curry. Scatter over chopped parsley and cilantro, cashews, or pumpkin seeds.

peruvian bowl

Serves 4

¾ cup (5 oz./130 g) dried red beans
4 tbsp (60 ml) olive oil
1 large garlic clove, peeled and finely chopped
1 celery stalk, washed and finely chopped
1 red onion, peeled and finely chopped
1 red bell pepper (optional), washed, seeded, and diced
3 cups (750 ml) water
2 bay leaves, washed
1 sprig fresh thyme, washed
1 tsp cumin seeds
1 tsp paprika

2 small or 1 large sweet potato, peeled and cut into cubes
3 oz. (75 g) kale, washed and shredded
Scant 1 cup (6 oz./160 g) quinoa
Scant 1 cup (6 oz./160 g) brown rice
1 tbsp (10 g) pumpkin seeds
1 tbsp (10 g) sunflower seeds
1 tbsp (15 ml) lemon juice
Salt and pepper
To serve:
A few flat-leaf parsley and cilantro leaves, washed
5 oz. (140 g) pico de gallo (recipe p. 222)

1 Soak the dried beans in a bowl of cold water overnight or for at least 10 hours. Drain and put the beans in a large saucepan of fresh water, bring to a boil, boil for 10 minutes, and then lower the heat and simmer for about 1 hour 30 minutes, or until the beans are tender. Drain. Preheat the oven to 350°F (180°C/Gas mark 4).

2 Heat 1 tbsp (15 ml) of the oil in a large saucepan over low heat and fry the garlic, celery, and red onion until the onion is translucent. Add the diced bell pepper and cook for about 10 minutes, until softened. Add the water, bay leaves, thyme, and spices. Meanwhile, drizzle the sweet potato cubes with 2 tbsp (30 ml) of the oil and roast in the oven for 20 minutes. Add the red beans, sweet potato, and kale to the saucepan and simmer until the vegetables are very tender.

3 While the vegetables are simmering, rinse the quinoa and rice under running water. Cook in separate saucepans of boiling, salted water—10 minutes for the quinoa and about 30 minutes for the rice—until tender. Drain and transfer the quinoa and rice to a bowl, stir in the seeds, lemon juice, and remaining 1 tbsp (15 ml) olive oil, and mix well. Season with salt and pepper. Remove the bay leaves and serve the vegetables with the rice and quinoa. Scatter over the parsley and cilantro and accompany each serving with a generous spoonful of pico de gallo.

chili sin carne

Serves 4

Scant 1¼ cups (9 oz./250 g) dried red beans
1 garlic clove, peeled and finely chopped
1 onion, peeled and finely chopped
A little olive oil for frying
5 tbsp (80 g) tomato paste
2 large eggplants, washed and cut into small cubes
2 red bell peppers, washed, seeded, and cut into small cubes
1 lb. (450 g) button mushrooms, washed and chopped
4 ripe tomatoes, washed and chopped
⅔ cup (160 ml) water
1 tsp paprika
½ tsp mild chili powder
1 bay leaf, washed
Salt and pepper
To serve:
4 tbsp (60 g) vegan cream cheese (recipe p. 227)
4 tbsp (60 g) pico de gallo (recipe p. 222)
Lime wedges

 Soak the dried beans in a bowl of cold water overnight or for at least 10 hours. Drain and put the beans in a large saucepan of fresh, salted water. Bring to a boil, boil for 10 minutes, lower the heat, and simmer for 1 hour 30 minutes or until the beans are tender. Drain.

 Fry the garlic and onion in a little olive oil in a large saucepan over low heat. Stir in the tomato paste and all the vegetables and continue frying. Pour in the water and add the spices, bay leaf, and red beans. Bring to a simmer and continue cooking until all the vegetables are tender.

 Remove and discard the bay leaf and season with salt and pepper. Divide among 4 plates and accompany each serving with a tbsp of vegan cream cheese and pico de gallo. Accompany with lime wedges to squeeze over.

wild tacos

Serves 4

---

1 avocado, halved, pitted, and peeled
12 small gluten-free corn tacos
1 quantity pico de gallo (recipe p. 222)
4 servings chili sin carne (recipe p. 76)
Vegan cream cheese (recipe p. 227)
½ tsp paprika
A few cilantro sprigs, washed
Fine slices of red onion
To serve:
Lime
Sumac

 Cut the avocado flesh into slices.

 Warm the tacos in a dry skillet or in the oven. In the center of each taco, place a spoonful of pico de gallo, a large spoonful of chili sin carne, an avocado slice, a little cream cheese with paprika (add ½ tsp paprika to the recipe p. 227), a cilantro sprig, and some red onion slices. Squeeze over lime juice and dust with a pinch of sumac.

pasta o'pesto

Serves 4

14 oz. (400 g) soba noodles
1 tbsp plus 1 tsp (20 ml) sesame oil
A drizzle of coconut oil
½-in. (1-cm) piece fresh ginger, peeled and finely chopped
2 small scallions, washed and finely chopped
1 tbsp (15 ml) tamari
5 oz. (150 g) basil pesto (recipe p. 227)
1½ tbsp (15 g) pine nuts, toasted
Salt and pepper
To serve:
A few sprigs purple Sakura cress, washed
Lime wedges

1 Cook the noodles in a large saucepan of boiling, salted water for 5 minutes. As soon as they are cooked, drain the noodles, and immerse them in a bowl of cold water. Drain again, place the noodles in a salad bowl, and toss with the sesame oil. Chill in the refrigerator until ready to serve.

2 Heat the coconut oil in a large skillet and add the ginger. Season with salt and pepper, cover the pan, and cook over low heat for 5 minutes. Add the scallions and cook for a few more minutes. Add the tamari, stir well, and remove from the heat.

3 Mix the noodles with the sautéed ginger, scallions, and pesto. Divide between 4 wide shallow bowls and scatter over the pine nuts. Serve the noodles topped with a few sprigs of Sakura cress, accompanied by a fresh salad and lime wedges to squeeze over.

#salads

. . . .

Crunchy, crisp, bursting with color, life, and energy, salads are a daily necessity for me. What I like most about them is their potential for infinite variety, using all sorts of combinations. Here are some of my favorite recipes that are particularly rich in sprouts and seeds.

earth bowl

. . . .

Serves 4

———

2 eggplants, washed and cut into large cubes
1 quantity bò bún sauce (recipe p. 222)
Generous 1 cup (9 oz./250 g) brown round rice
2 tbsp (30 ml) beet juice
1 tbsp (15 ml) toasted sesame oil
1 tbsp (15 ml) rice vinegar
1 ripe mango, peeled and flesh cut into julienne strips
½ black radish, peeled and cut into julienne strips
1 tbsp plus 1 tsp (20 ml) citrus vinaigrette (recipe p. 223)
4½ oz. (120 g) edamame
Salt and pepper
To serve:
Black sesame seeds
Miso mayonnaise (recipe p. 224)
A few small flat-leaf parsley sprigs, washed

1 Preheat the oven to 350°F (180°C/Gas mark 4). In a bowl, mix the eggplant cubes with the bò bún sauce until coated, spread the cubes out on a baking sheet, and roast in the oven for about 30 minutes, until tender and golden brown.

2 Meanwhile, cook the rice in a large saucepan of boiling, salted water until tender. Drain the rice and stir in the beet juice to color the grains evenly. Season with half the sesame oil, the rice vinegar, salt, and pepper. Drizzle the mango and radish strips with the citrus vinaigrette. Combine the edamame with the remaining sesame oil and season with salt and pepper.

3 To serve, divide the beet-colored rice between 4 bowls, add the roasted eggplants, edamame, and then the mango and radish julienne. Serve sprinkled with black sesame seeds and flat-leaf parsley sprigs, and accompany with miso mayonnaise.

green bowl

Serves 4

1 black radish, peeled and cut into julienne strips
1 cucumber, peeled, seeded, and cut into julienne strips
3 tbsp (45 ml) olive oil
1 tbsp (15 ml) cider vinegar
1 small head broccoli, washed and cut into florets
6 oz. (160 g) green beans, washed and trimmed
2 small shallots, peeled and finely chopped
1 handful baby spinach leaves, washed
2 small avocados, halved and pitted
1½ tsp poppy seeds
1 pinch gomasio
Salt and pepper
To serve:
1 quantity spirulina sauce (recipe p. 223)
Sunflower seeds
Fresh mint leaves (or fresh herbs of your choice), washed and chopped
A few cooked chickpeas
Pumpkin seeds

 Season the radish and cucumber strips with salt and pepper and drizzle with a little of the olive oil and the cider vinegar. Cook the broccoli florets in a saucepan of boiling, salted water for 2 minutes, just until al dente. Drain the broccoli and immediately immerse the florets in a bowl of ice water.

 Cook the green beans in the same way for 7–10 minutes, then drain and immerse in a bowl of ice water. Drain the broccoli and beans and season with the remaining olive oil, shallots, salt, and pepper.

 To serve, divide the julienned vegetables and spinach leaves between 4 plates and add the broccoli and beans. Arrange the avocado halves alongside and scatter over the poppy seeds and gomasio. Add a generous spoonful of spirulina sauce in the center of each bowl or serve separately. Scatter over sunflower seeds, chopped mint, cooked chickpeas, and pumpkin seeds.

protein bowl

Serves 4

———

2⅓ cups (14 oz./400 g) quinoa
1 cucumber, washed and halved lengthwise
⅔ oz. (20 g) nori seaweed, chopped
2 scallions, washed and chopped
3 oz. (80 g) edamame
Seeds of 1 pomegranate
3 tbsp (45 ml) olive oil
A squeeze of lemon juice
Salt
To serve:
2 avocados, halved and pitted
A few arugula leaves, washed
4 tbsp (60 g) white cashew sauce (recipe p. 224)
1 scallion, washed and chopped

1 Cook the quinoa in a saucepan of boiling, salted water for 10 minutes. While it is cooking, cut the cucumber halves into ¼-in. (5-mm) slices.

2 Drain the quinoa, let cool, and place in a mixing bowl. Add the seaweed, chopped scallions, edamame, pomegranate seeds, and cucumber slices. Dress with the olive oil and lemon juice. Season with salt and stir lightly to combine the ingredients evenly.

3 Serve the salad in 4 shallow bowls, accompanied by the avocado halves and arugula leaves, topped with 1 tbsp of white cashew sauce. Sprinkle with the chopped scallion.

bò bún

Serves 4

——

1 lb. (500 g) rice vermicelli noodles
½ napa cabbage, washed and finely shredded
2 carrots, peeled and cut into julienne strips
1 small cucumber, washed, seeded, and grated
A few mint leaves, washed and chopped
A few cilantro leaves, washed and chopped
2 tbsp (20 g) raw peanuts, toasted
3 oz. (80 g) bò bún sauce (recipe p. 222)
2 shallots, peeled and finely sliced
A drizzle of olive oil
To serve:
4 tbsp (40 g) raw peanuts, chopped and toasted
4 tofu skewers marinated in bò bún sauce

1 Rinse the noodles thoroughly in cold water and then drain well.

2 Mix the noodles with the shredded cabbage, carrot strips, grated cucumber, chopped herbs, peanuts, and bò bún sauce. Fry the shallots in the olive oil until golden.

3 Divide between individual dishes and serve sprinkled with the fried shallots and toasted peanuts. Accompany each serving with a tofu skewer marinated in bò bún sauce.

soba noodles

Serves 4

---

9 oz. (250 g) butternut squash, peeled, seeds and fibers removed
A drizzle of olive oil
10 oz. (280 g) soba noodles
1 tbsp (15 g) curry powder
1 garlic clove, peeled and chopped
2 tbsp (40 g) maple syrup
½-in. (1-cm) piece fresh ginger, peeled and finely chopped
¾ cup (200 ml) coconut milk
2 handfuls baby spinach leaves, washed
3 oz. (80 g) kale, washed and shredded
3 tbsp (40 g) coconut oil
Salt and pepper
To serve:
1 red onion, peeled and finely chopped
1½ oz. (40 g) basil leaves, washed
2 tbsp (20 g) hemp seeds
1½ oz. (40 g) almonds, chopped

1 Preheat the oven to 350°F (180°C/Gas mark 4). Cut the squash into cubes and toss them in the olive oil until coated. Spread out the squash on a baking sheet lined with parchment paper and roast in the oven for 25–30 minutes until tender, but keep an eye on the cubes to check they do not brown too much.

2 Meanwhile, cook the noodles in a large saucepan of boiling, salted water for 3 minutes and then drain. Prepare the sauce by blending the curry powder, garlic, maple syrup, ginger, and coconut milk together. Mix the noodles with the sauce until they are coated and season with salt and pepper.

3 Quickly sauté the spinach leaves and kale in the coconut oil. Divide the spinach and kale between 4 serving plates and top with the noodles and squash. Scatter over the chopped onion, basil leaves, hemp seeds, and chopped almonds.

rawliflower

Serves 4

———

1 small cauliflower, washed
2 red apples, washed, cored, and cut into sticks
2 tbsp (30 ml) lemon juice
7 oz. (200 g) vegan blue cheese
6 tbsp (90 ml) olive oil
1 tbsp (15 ml) cider vinegar
¼ red cabbage, washed and finely shredded
1 good handful walnuts, roughly chopped
3½ oz. (100 g) pomegranate seeds
20 mint leaves, washed and chopped
20 flat-leaf parsley leaves, washed and chopped
20 chive stems, washed and chopped
Salt and pepper
To serve (optional):
Edible flowers, washed

1 Finely grate the cauliflower so it has the texture of tabbouleh grains.
Toss the apple sticks with the lemon juice to prevent them discoloring.
Cut the vegan blue cheese into bite-sized cubes.

2 Make a dressing with the olive oil and cider vinegar and season with salt
and pepper. In a bowl, lightly mix together the cauliflower, apple sticks,
red cabbage, walnuts, pomegranate seeds, chopped herbs, and the dressing.
Season with salt and pepper.

3 Divide the salad between 4 serving plates and add the cheese cubes to
each one. Garnish with a few edible flowers, if using.

crisp brussels sprouts

Serves 4

---

3 tbsp (45 ml) water
3 tbsp (45 ml) cider vinegar
6 tbsp (90 ml) olive oil
1 tbsp (15 g) French mustard
1 tbsp (20 g) maple syrup
9 oz. (250 g) Brussels sprouts, washed and very thinly sliced
1½ oz. (40 g) fresh peas
1½ oz. (40 g) dried cranberries
1 pinch black pepper
To serve:
Generous ⅓ cup (2 oz./60 g) toasted pecans, roughly chopped
A few sprigs purple Sakura cress, washed

1 Make the dressing by whisking together the water, vinegar, olive oil, mustard, and maple syrup in a large bowl until evenly combined.

2 Add all the remaining ingredients to the dressing.

3 Divide between 4 serving bowls and scatter over the pecans and some sprigs of purple cress.

the kale salad

Serves 4

——

1 tbsp (15 ml) cider vinegar
3 tbsp (45 ml) sesame oil
1 tbsp (15 g) French mustard
2 tbsp (40 g) maple syrup, divided
10 large kale leaves, washed and shredded
1 red onion, peeled and halved
1 small sweet potato, peeled and halved
1 small red-skinned apple, washed and cored
4 pink radishes, washed
1 small beet, washed
2 tbsp (20 g) almonds
1 pinch Cayenne pepper
A few sprigs purple Sakura cress, alfalfa sprouts,
  and pea shoots, washed
Salt and pepper

1 Make a dressing by whisking together the vinegar, sesame oil, mustard, and 1 tbsp (20 g) of the maple syrup until evenly combined. Season with salt and pepper.

2 Steam the kale for 5 minutes and, as soon as it is wilted, immerse it in a bowl of ice water. Using a mandolin or sharp knife, cut the onion halves, sweet potato halves, apple, radishes, and beet into very thin slices.

3 Toss the almonds with the remaining 1 tbsp (20 g) of maple syrup and the Cayenne pepper and toast in a small skillet until golden. Let the almonds cool on a sheet of parchment paper and then chop into small pieces. Divide everything between 4 bowls, pour over the dressing, and scatter with Sakura cress, alfalfa sprouts, and pea shoots.

raw beet & ginger

Serves 4

———

3½ oz. (100 g) red beet, washed
3½ oz. (100 g) yellow beet, washed
3½ oz. (100 g) chioggia beet, washed
1 red-skinned apple, washed and cored
Scant ½ cup (2 oz./60 g) hazelnuts
1 cup (20 g) arugula, washed
½-in. (1-cm) piece fresh ginger, peeled and finely chopped
Juice of 1 lemon
2 tbsp (30 ml) olive oil
3 tbsp (45 ml) hazelnut oil
A few sprigs purple Sakura cress (optional), washed

1 Using a mandolin or sharp knife, cut the beets and apple into thin slices. Toast the hazelnuts in a skillet and then roughly chop them.

2 Divide the beet slices, apple slices, and arugula between 4 serving bowls.

3 Make the dressing by blending together the ginger, lemon juice, and oils. Drizzle the dressing over the salads and scatter the chopped hazelnuts and Sakura cress, if using, on top.

greek salad, our style

Serves 4

1 cucumber, washed and halved lengthwise
1 oz. (30 g) pitted black olives, roughly chopped
3 tbsp (45 ml) olive oil
1 tbsp (15 ml) lemon juice
3½ oz. (100 g) vegan feta-style cheese
3 large handfuls lamb's lettuce, washed
1 bunch flat-leaf parsley, washed and chopped
2 small scallions, washed and chopped
Generous ½ cup (3 oz./80 g) almonds, toasted and chopped
Salt and pepper

1 Cut each cucumber half into thin slices using a mandolin or sharp knife and season with salt and pepper.

2 Preheat the oven to 500°F (260°C/Gas mark 10). Spread out the chopped olives on a baking sheet and put them in the oven for 5 minutes. Make a dressing by whisking together the olive oil and lemon juice. Crumble the vegan feta-style cheese into small pieces.

3 Mix all the ingredients together in a large bowl, pour over the dressing, and season with salt and pepper.

seaweed guac

Serves 4

For the guacamole:
4 avocados, halved and pitted
1 small white onion, peeled and finely chopped
1 garlic clove, peeled and finely chopped
Juice of 1 lemon
2 tbsp (30 ml) olive oil
Salt and pepper
For the seaweed tartare:
1 oz. (30 g) dried seaweed
1 shallot, peeled and finely chopped
10 gherkins, sliced lengthwise
2 tbsp (20 g) capers
1 tbsp (15 ml) lemon juice, plus a little extra to drizzle

1 Prepare the guacamole by using a spoon to scoop out the flesh of the avocados, and then mash it roughly. Add the onion and garlic to the avocado flesh with the lemon juice and olive oil. Season with salt and pepper, and mix well.

2 Prepare the seaweed tartare by soaking the seaweed to rehydrate it and then drain, rinse, and chop it. Stir the shallot into the seaweed with the gherkins and capers. Add the lemon juice and stir until evenly combined.

3 Divide the guacamole between 4 serving dishes and add the seaweed tartare. Drizzle a few drops of lemon juice over each serving.

cucumber & wakame

Serves 4

—

1¾ oz. (50 g) dried wakame
1 large cucumber, washed and halved lengthwise
½-in. (1-cm) piece fresh ginger, peeled and grated
2 tbsp (30 ml) sesame oil
1 tbsp (15 ml) rice vinegar
1 tbsp (15 ml) umeboshi (ume plum) vinegar
2 tbsp (30 ml) tamari
½ red onion, peeled and thinly sliced
To serve:
Cilantro leaves, washed and finely chopped, or black sesame seeds
Edible flowers (optional), washed

 Soak the wakame in a bowl of hot water for 20 minutes. Drain, rinse, and tear into small strips. Using a mandolin or sharp knife, cut the cucumber halves into thin half-moon slices.

 Mix the ginger with the sesame oil, rice vinegar, umeboshi vinegar, and tamari, to make a dressing.

 Pour the dressing over the cucumber slices, wakame, and sliced onion and toss well. Divide between 4 plates and sprinkle with chopped cilantro leaves or black sesame seeds, and edible flowers, if using.

#desserts

. . . .

No doubt, you'll have noticed that this is one
of the longest chapters in the book. Challenging
preconceptions, we aim to prove that healthy eating
doesn't have to mean skimping on sweet treats.
Quite the contrary, they just need to be rethought.
We've included plenty of super ingredients, focusing
on natural sweeteners and gentle cooking.
Our desserts are proof that healthy can be fun, too.

super glow salad

Serves 4

—

1 small handful goji berries
Juice of 1 orange
1 papaya
8 mangosteen
1 large avocado, halved, pitted, and peeled
1 pomegranate

1 Soak the goji berries in the orange juice to rehydrate them. Halve the papaya lengthwise, peel, and scoop out the seeds with a spoon. Wash, cut around the middle of each mangosteen with a sharp knife, peel away the thick skin, and remove the white flesh inside.

2 Chop the papaya and avocado into cubes and separate the mangosteen flesh into segments. Cut around the middle of the pomegranate, pull apart, and hold each half upside down over a bowl. Tap with a wooden spoon to release the seeds.

3 Gently mix the prepared fruits together in a bowl and pour over the orange juice and goji berries.

acai coco loco

Serves 4

⅔ cup (3 oz./80 g) cashews
3 tbsp (60 g) maple syrup
1 pinch ground vanilla bean
¾ cup (200 ml) coconut milk
1 tsp (2 g) agar agar
2 cups plus 2 tbsp (500 ml) boiling water
1 tbsp (15 g) acai powder
1 tbsp plus 1 tsp (20 ml) lemon juice
To serve:
2 oz. (50 g) seeds of your choice or unsweetened shredded coconut
Fresh blueberries, washed

1 Soak the cashews in a bowl of cold water for 8 hours or overnight. Drain and rinse well. Blend the maple syrup, cashews, vanilla, and coconut milk together until smooth and creamy. Divide between 4 serving dishes and refrigerate.

2 To make the acai jelly, dissolve the agar agar in the boiling water (follow the package instructions), and then blend with the acai powder and lemon juice. Chill in the refrigerator for at least 2 hours.

3 Divide the jelly between the dishes, swirling it with the coconut milk mixture. Sprinkle with seeds of your choice or shredded coconut, and accompany with fresh blueberries.

banana bread

Makes 1 loaf

1½ oz. (40 g) chia seeds
¾ cup (185 ml) almond mylk (recipe p. 218)
6 very ripe bananas, peeled and roughly chopped
⅓ cup (2½ oz./70 g) coconut oil, plus extra for greasing the loaf pan
⅔ cup (3½ oz./100 g) white rice flour
⅔ cup (3½ oz./100 g) cornstarch
1 tbsp (15 g) gluten-free baking powder
1½ oz. (40 g) buckwheat flakes
2¼ cups (6 oz./170 g) unsweetened shredded coconut
1 tsp ground cinnamon
1 tsp ground vanilla bean
1 pinch nutmeg
½ cup (2½ oz./65 g) hazelnuts, roughly chopped
3½ tbsp (70 g) maple syrup
To serve:
Vanilla cream (recipe p. 221)
1 tsp poppy seeds

 Preheat the oven to 325°F (160°C/Gas mark 3). Soak the chia seeds in the almond mylk for 20 minutes.

 Using a fork or potato masher, roughly mash the bananas with the coconut oil. Add all the other ingredients to the mashed bananas, including the chia seeds and almond mylk, mixing well. Grease a large loaf pan with coconut oil and line with parchment paper. Pour the batter into the pan and bake for 35 minutes, or until a cake tester pushed into the center comes out clean.

 Once the banana bread is cooked, remove it from the oven and let cool in the pan before turning it out. Accompany with vanilla cream sprinkled with the poppy seeds.

Note: If there is any banana bread left over the next day, it's delicious toasted for breakfast!

wild muesli

. . . .

Serves 1

────

¾ oz. (20 g) gluten-free rolled oats
1 tbsp (10 g) chia seeds
1 tbsp (10 g) raisins
4 tbsp (60 ml) almond mylk (recipe p. 218) or
    other plant-based mylk, heated
1 tbsp (20 g) maple syrup
1 pinch ground cinnamon
To serve:
1 red-skinned apple, washed and chopped
A few pumpkin seeds, toasted
Chopped walnuts
Banana slices
Ground cinnamon

 Soak the oats, chia seeds, and raisins in the hot mylk and maple syrup
for 20 minutes. Stir in the cinnamon.

 Spoon the muesli into a bowl and serve with the chopped apple, toasted
pumpkin seeds, chopped walnuts, banana slices, and a sprinkle of ground
cinnamon.

*Note: You can eat the muesli hot or it can be chilled in the refrigerator
to enjoy the next day, accompanied by a glass of almond mylk.*

banana crumble

Serves 5

———

1¼ cups (4½ oz./125 g) ground almonds
Generous 1 cup (3 oz./85 g) unsweetened shredded coconut
1¾ oz. (50 g) coconut sugar
1 tbsp (12.5 g) coconut oil
1 pinch salt
5 very ripe bananas, peeled
2 tbsp (30 ml) coconut milk
1 pinch ground vanilla bean
To serve:
Pomegranate seeds

1 Preheat the oven to 325°F (170°C/Gas mark 3). Line a baking sheet with parchment paper. Process the ground almonds, shredded coconut, sugar, coconut oil, and salt together to obtain a crumbly texture. Spread the crumble in an even, but not too thick layer over the baking sheet and bake in the oven for 10–15 minutes, keeping an eye on it as it cooks so that it does not burn.

2 When the crumble has turned a golden color, remove it from the oven and let cool. Meanwhile, use a fork to mash the bananas with the coconut milk and vanilla.

3 Break the crumble into small pieces. Divide the bananas between 5 individual dishes and cover with a layer of crumble. Serve with pomegranate seeds scattered over.

blueberry scones

Makes 6

½ cup (9 oz./250 g) rice flour
2½ cups (9 oz./250 g) ground almonds
¾ tsp gluten-free baking powder
¾ tsp baking soda
1 large pinch ground vanilla bean
1 pinch salt
1 tbsp plus 2 tsp (25 ml) coconut milk
1 tbsp plus 2 tsp (25 ml) almond mylk (recipe p. 218)
3 tbsp (60 g) maple syrup
2 oz. (60 g) frozen blueberries
To serve:
Vanilla cream (recipe p. 221)
Blueberries, washed

1 Preheat the oven to 300°F (150°C/Gas mark 2). Line a baking sheet with parchment paper. Mix together the rice flour, ground almonds, baking powder, baking soda, vanilla, and salt. Stir in the coconut milk, almond mylk, and maple syrup. Mix lightly until the ingredients come together to make a soft dough. Stir in the blueberries to marble the dough.

2 Roll out the dough on a lightly floured board to a thickness of 2 in. (5 cm), and, using an approximately 2½-in. (6–7-cm) round cookie cutter, cut out 6 scones. Place them on the lined baking sheet and bake for 15 minutes, or until well risen and golden brown.

3 Remove the scones from the oven and let cool on a rack for 2 hours. Serve with vanilla cream and blueberries.

chia pudding

Serves 4

3½ oz. (100 g) chia seeds
1⅔ cups (400 ml) barista mylk (recipe p. 220) or coconut milk
1 tbsp (15 ml) orange blossom water
2 tbsp (40 g) maple syrup
1 pinch ground vanilla bean
To serve:
Pitted black cherries
1 tbsp (5 g) unsweetened shredded coconut
A few chopped pistachios

1   Soak the chia seeds in the barista mylk or coconut milk for at least 30 minutes, stirring them occasionally to prevent the mixture becoming too thick.

2   Lightly stir the soaked chia seeds into the remaining ingredients. Warm the cherries slightly so they release their juice and stir them in.

3   Divide between 4 bowls and serve sprinkled with the shredded coconut and chopped pistachios.

raw chocolate tart

Serves 12
___

For the crust:
7 oz. (200 g) date paste
Scant 1 cup (6 oz./160 g) toasted hazelnuts
3½ oz. (100 g) gluten-free rolled oats
1 tbsp plus 1 tsp (15 g) coconut oil
1 pinch salt
1 pinch ground cinnamon
For the filling:
1½ cups (9 oz./250 g) cashews, pre-soaked in cold water for 8 hours
⅓ cup (2½ oz./70 g) coconut oil
3½ tbsp (70 g) maple syrup
Scant ½ cup (1¾ oz./50 g) unsweetened cocoa powder
⅔ cup (150 ml) water
1 pinch ground vanilla bean
1 pinch ground cinnamon
3 oz. (75 g) vegan dark chocolate
To serve:
Unsweetened shredded coconut for sprinkling
Edible flowers, washed

 To make the crust, blend all the ingredients together until they resemble coarse crumbs. Press the crumbs together with your hands to make a dough, shape it into a ball, and roll out into a round large enough to line an 11-in. (28-cm) tart pan or tart ring set on a cookie sheet. Chill in the refrigerator while you prepare the filling.

 To make the filling, drain the cashews and rinse well. Process all the ingredients together, except the chocolate, until smooth and creamy. Chop the chocolate and melt it in a bain-marie or a bowl set over a pan of just simmering water. When melted, stir until smooth and then gradually fold it into the creamy mixture with a spatula. Spread the filling evenly over the chilled crust and return to the refrigerator for 30 minutes.

 Serve the tart sprinkled with shredded coconut and decorated with a few edible flowers.

orange blossom cookies

Makes about 10

2 cups (7 oz./200 g) ground almonds
1⅓ cups (7 oz./200 g) white rice flour
½ tsp salt
1 tbsp plus 1 tsp (20 ml) orange blossom water
Generous ¾ cup (7 oz./200 g) maple syrup
¾ cup (200 ml) almond mylk (recipe p. 218)
8 oz. (230 g) white almond butter
3 oz. (80 g) pistachios and/or pecans, roughly chopped

1 Mix the ground almonds, rice flour, and salt together in a mixing bowl. Add the orange blossom water, maple syrup, almond mylk, and almond butter, and mix to make a dough.

2 Preheat the oven to 350°F (180°C/Gas mark 4). Line a baking sheet with parchment paper. Divide the dough into 10 pieces and roll into balls. Press the balls into the chopped pistachios or pecans so the nuts stick to them. Place the cookies, nuts side up, on the lined baking sheet.

3 Bake the cookies for 15 minutes, remove from the oven, and let cool on a wire rack.

lemon tart

Serves 12

___

For the crust:
1¾ cups (6 oz./170 g) ground almonds
8 oz. (220 g) date paste
1 pinch salt
For the filling:
8 oz. (220 g) date paste
1 cup plus 2 tbsp (275 ml) lemon juice
⅓ cup (2½ oz./70 g) coconut oil
⅓ cup plus 1 tsp (85 ml) coconut milk
1½ oz. (40 g) finely grated lemon zest
Scant ¾ cup (190 ml) water
2⅔ cups (7 oz./200 g) unsweetened shredded coconut
To serve:
Finely grated lemon zest
Chopped pistachios

 To make the crust, blend the ground almonds, date paste, and salt together until the mixture resembles coarse crumbs. Press the crumbs together with your hands to make a dough and shape into a smooth ball. Roll out the dough, line the base of an 11-in. (28-cm) tart pan or tart ring set on a cookie sheet, and chill in the refrigerator while you prepare the filling.

 To make the filling, blend all the ingredients together, except the shredded coconut, until smooth and creamy. Add the coconut and process again until combined. Spread the filling evenly over the tart base and chill in the refrigerator for 30 minutes.

 To serve, sprinkle the tart with lemon zest and chopped pistachios.

matchia pudding

Serves 4
—

3½ oz. (100 g) chia seeds
1⅔ cups (400 ml) barista mylk (recipe p. 220) or coconut milk
1 tbsp (6 g) matcha green tea powder
1 pinch ground vanilla bean
2 tbsp (40 g) maple syrup
To serve:
1 banana, peeled and sliced
Grated fresh coconut
Toasted pumpkin seeds
3½ oz. (100 g) date paste (optional)

1 Soak the chia seeds in the barista mylk or coconut milk for at least 30 minutes, stirring them occasionally to prevent the mixture becoming too thick.

2 Add the remaining ingredients and stir everything together lightly.

3 Serve in individual bowls, topped with the banana slices, grated coconut, and toasted pumpkin seeds. Accompany each serving with a spoonful of date paste, if wished.

Note: You can replace the banana slices with raspberries or another fruit in season.

pom'pot

Serves 4

——

4 large Golden Delicious apples, peeled and cored
½ cup (120 ml) water
Juice of ½ lemon
To serve:
1 quantity vanilla cream (recipe p. 221)
Ground cinnamon

1 Chop the apples into chunks. Simmer them with the water and lemon juice in a saucepan over low heat for 20–30 minutes, until tender.

2 Spoon the apple compote into individual bowls and cover with a layer of vanilla cream. Serve sprinkled with a little ground cinnamon.

poached pears

Serves 4

For the pears:
2 large pears
¾ cup (200 ml) water
⅔ oz. (20 g) coconut sugar
1 pinch ground vanilla bean
For the praline:
2½ tbsp (20 g) hazelnuts
1 tsp coconut sugar
1 pinch salt
To serve:
4 tbsp (60 g) vanilla cream (recipe p. 221)
Chopped pistachios

1 To prepare the poached pears, remove the stalks and peel the pears, leaving them whole. Make a syrup by heating the water, sugar, and vanilla in a saucepan, stirring until the sugar dissolves. Bring to a boil, then reduce the heat to low and add the pears. Cover with a lid and poach gently for 30 minutes. Lift out the pears with a slotted spoon, transfer to a bowl, and pour over the poaching syrup. Let cool.

2 To make the praline, preheat the oven to 300°F (150°C/Gas mark 2). Spread out the hazelnuts on a baking sheet and roast for 20 minutes. Process with the coconut sugar and salt until finely ground.

3 To serve, halve the pears and remove the cores. Place 1 generous tbsp of vanilla cream on each serving plate and sit a pear half on top, rounded side down. Fill the pear hollows with a scoop of praline and scatter over chopped pistachios.

strawberry coco loco

Serves 4

Scant ½ cup (3 oz./80 g) cashews
3 tbsp (60 g) maple syrup
1 pinch ground vanilla bean
¾ cup (200 ml) coconut milk
1 tsp (2 g) agar agar
2 cups plus 2 tbsp (500 ml) boiling water
8 oz. (240 g) strawberries, washed
Juice of ½ lemon
To serve (optional):
2 oz. (50 g) grated fresh coconut
Fresh strawberries, washed

1 Soak the cashews in a bowl of cold water for 8 hours or overnight. Drain and rinse well. Blend the maple syrup, cashews, vanilla, and coconut milk together until smooth and creamy. Divide between individual plates and chill in the refrigerator.

2 To make the strawberry jelly, dissolve the agar agar in the boiling water (follow the package instructions). Blend with the strawberries and lemon juice and chill in the refrigerator for at least 2 hours.

3 Divide the jelly between the serving plates and swirl with the creamy coconut mixture. Sprinkle with the grated coconut and decorate with fresh strawberries, if desired.

raw vegan cheesecake

Serves 14

---

3 cups (1 lb./500 g) cashews
For the crust:
1⅔ cups (9 oz./250 g) almonds, roughly chopped
¾ oz. (20 g) fresh coconut, chopped
4½ oz. (130 g) date paste
For the filling:
⅔ cup (150 ml) lemon juice
½ cup (3½ oz./100 g) coconut oil
¾ cup (9 oz./ 250 g) maple syrup
1 pinch salt
1 tsp ground vanilla bean
For the blueberry compote:
3½ oz. (100 g) frozen blueberries
1 tbsp (20 g) maple syrup
To serve:
Mint sprigs

1 Soak the cashews in a bowl of cold water for 8 hours or overnight. Drain, rinse well, and set aside for the filling.

2 To make the crust, blend all the ingredients together. Press the mixture in an even layer over the base of a 12-in. (30-cm) tart pan. Chill in the refrigerator while you make the filling.

3 To make the filling, blend all the ingredients together with the soaked cashews. Spread the mixture evenly over the crust and return to the refrigerator to chill again.

4 To make the blueberry compote, simmer the blueberries and maple syrup in a saucepan over gentle heat for about 10 minutes, stirring regularly, until thickened. Let cool. Spread the compote over the filling just before serving. Decorate with mint sprigs.

matcha nice cream

Makes 8 scoops

1⅔ cups (9 oz./250 g) cashews
⅓ cup (1½ oz./45 g) almonds
1¼ cups (300 ml) almond mylk (recipe p. 218)
1¼ cups (300 ml) water
1¾ oz. (50 g) date paste
⅓ cup (3½ oz./100 g) maple syrup
1 avocado, flesh removed and chopped
5 tsp matcha green tea powder
¼ cup (10 g) roughly chopped mint leaves
1½ tbsp (10 g) roughly chopped pistachios
To serve:
Small mint sprigs, washed

 Soak the cashews and almonds in a bowl of cold water for 8 hours or overnight. Drain and rinse well. Process all the ingredients together until smooth and creamy. Transfer the mixture to the beakers of a Pacojet®, before putting in the freezer for a minimum of 24 hours.

 The following day, take the beakers out of the freezer and pacotize® twice. You can also make this frozen cream in an ice-cream maker. To do this, prepare the mixture as in step 1, pour it into the ice-cream maker, and churn according to the manufacturer's instructions. Transfer to a resealable container and freeze until ready to serve.

 Serve in scoops, decorating each serving with a mint sprig.

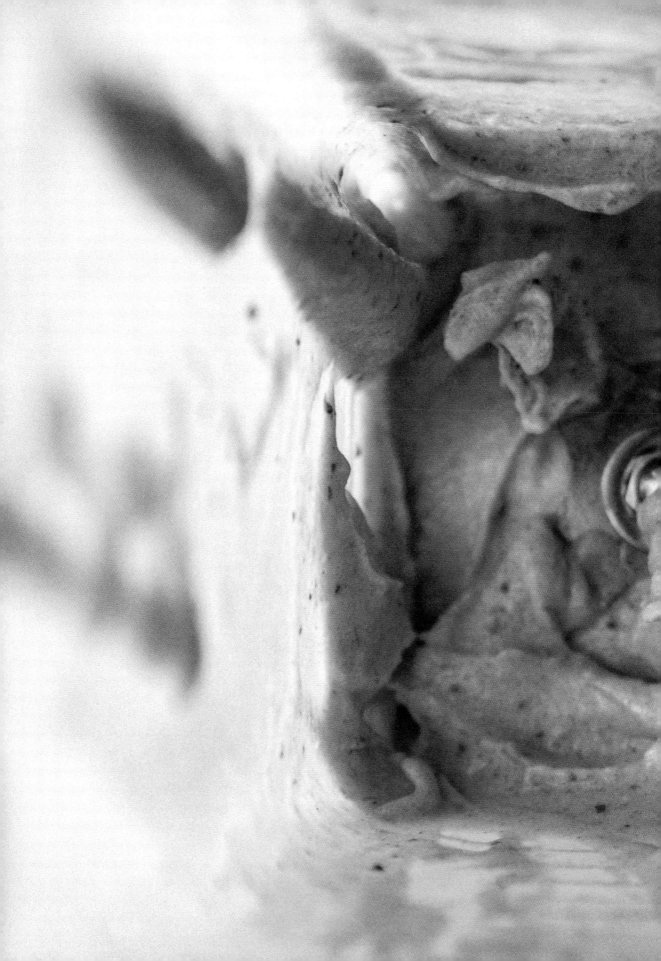

vanilla & thyme nice cream

Makes 8 scoops

—

1½ cups (9 oz./250 g) cashews
¾ cup (3½ oz./100 g) almonds
1 sprig fresh thyme, washed
1½ cups (350 ml) almond mylk (recipe p. 218)
1¼ cups (300 ml) water
⅓ cup (3½ oz./100 g) maple syrup
1 pinch ground vanilla bean
To serve:
Small thyme sprigs, washed

1 Soak the cashews and almonds in a bowl of cold water for 8 hours or overnight. Drain and rinse well. Pick the thyme leaves off the stalk. Blend all the ingredients together until smooth and creamy. Transfer the mixture to the beakers of a Pacojet®, before putting in the freezer for a minimum of 24 hours.

2 The following day, take the beakers out of the freezer and pacotize® twice. You can also make this frozen cream in an ice-cream maker. To do this, prepare the mixture as in step 1, pour it into the ice-cream maker, and churn according to the manufacturer's instructions. Transfer to a resealable container and freeze until ready to serve.

3 Serve in scoops, topped with small sprigs of thyme.

baked apples

Serves 4

—

3 oz. (80 g) almond butter
1½ tbsp (30 g) maple syrup
4 Golden Delicious apples, washed, cored and left whole
To serve:
Roughly chopped walnuts
Ground cinnamon

1 Preheat the oven to 350°F (180°C/Gas mark 4). Blend the almond butter and maple syrup together until soft and creamy.

2 Using a sharp knife, score three horizontal lines at regular intervals around each apple, only cutting through the skin. Stand the apples upright in an ovenproof dish and bake for 30–35 minutes until they are tender.

3 Cut each apple into four slices through the scored lines. Serve the apples hot with walnuts scattered over, topped with the almond butter and maple syrup, and dusted with cinnamon.

little choco pots

Serves 4

—

Generous 1 cup (6 oz./160 g) cashews
1½ tbsp (25 g) maple syrup
⅔ cup (160 ml) water
2 oz. (60 g) pitted dates
Generous ¼ cup (1 oz./30 g) unsweetened cocoa powder
To serve:
⅓ cup (1½ oz./40 g) hazelnuts, toasted and roughly chopped

1 Soak the cashews in a bowl of cold water for 8 hours or overnight. Drain and rinse well.

2 Blend the cashews, maple syrup, water, and dates together until smooth. Add the cocoa powder and blend until just incorporated.

3 Pour the chocolate cream into 4 glasses and serve with the hazelnuts scattered over.

#energy snacks

....

In need of a little comfort or an energy boost?
There are all sorts of reasons to indulge in a snack
but there's no need to resort to junk food.
From popcorn and bars to bite-sized treats,
Wild & the Moon proposes a multitude of funky yet
healthy snacks, both savory and sweet.

chocolate truffles

Makes about 10

———

1½ oz. (40 g) cocoa butter
1½ tbsp (10 g) unsweetened cocoa powder,
  plus 1 tbsp (7 g) for dusting
½ tsp ground vanilla bean
1 tsp coconut oil
1½ tbsp (10 g) cocoa nibs
1 pinch salt
1 cup (3½ oz./100 g) walnuts
1 cup (3½ oz./100 g) ground almonds
4½ oz. (120 g) date paste

1 Line a baking sheet with parchment paper. Heat the cocoa butter in a bain-marie or a bowl over a pan of simmering water until soft. Combine the cocoa powder, vanilla, softened cocoa butter, coconut oil, cocoa nibs, and salt in a mixing bowl.

2 Roughly chop the walnuts and process with the ground almonds. Add the date paste to the food processor and then incorporate the chocolate mixture until evenly combined.

3 Using a small ice-cream scoop, shape the mixture into 10 or so balls and release them onto the lined baking sheet. Chill for at least 1 hour.

4 When the truffles are well chilled, dust them with cocoa powder.

cloud truffles

Makes about 10

——

1½ oz. (40 g) cocoa butter
2 tbsp (15 g) cocoa nibs
1¼ cups (4½ oz./125 g) ground almonds
1 cup (4½ oz./125 g) walnuts
2 tbsp (15 g) unsweetened cocoa powder
1 pinch ground vanilla bean
1 pinch salt
2 tsp coconut oil
5 oz. (150 g) date paste
1 oz. (25 g) cashews, pre-soaked in cold water for 8 hours
1 pinch blue spirulina powder, plus extra for dusting

 Line a baking sheet with parchment paper. Process together one quarter of the cocoa butter, the cocoa nibs, ground almonds, walnuts, cocoa powder, vanilla, salt, coconut oil, and date paste.

 Using a small ice-cream scoop, shape the mixture into 10 or so balls, releasing them onto the lined baking sheet. Chill for at least 2 hours.

 While they are chilling, prepare the coating. Drain the cashews and rinse well. Melt the rest of the cocoa butter in a bain-marie or a bowl over a pan of simmering water, and then process it with the cashews and blue spirulina powder until smooth. Dip each truffle in the mixture until evenly coated, dust with a little extra spirulina powder, and return to the refrigerator until ready to serve.

cocomatcha

Makes about 10

Scant 1 cup (2½ oz./70 g) unsweetened shredded coconut
2 tsp coconut oil
1¼ tbsp (25 g) maple syrup
2 tbsp (30 ml) coconut milk
1 tbsp (10 g) chia seeds
1 tsp matcha green tea powder, plus extra for dusting
1 oz. (30 g) vegan dark chocolate

 Line a baking sheet with parchment paper. In a mixing bowl, combine all the ingredients, apart from the chocolate.

 Using a small ice-cream scoop, shape the mixture into 10 or so balls, releasing them onto the lined baking sheet. Chill the balls for at least 1 hour.

 Once they are well chilled, melt the chocolate and dip the bottom of each ball into the chocolate to cover in a thin layer. Place the balls back on the parchment paper and chill in the refrigerator until the chocolate is set.

coconut macarons

. . . .

Makes about 10
___

Scant 1 cup (2½ oz./70 g)
   unsweetened shredded coconut
1¼ cups (4½ oz./120 g) ground
   almonds
3 oz. (85g) date paste
½ tsp ground cinnamon

1 tsp lemon juice
Finely grated zest of ½ lemon
1 tsp coconut oil
½ tsp ground vanilla bean
½ tsp cornflower petals
1 pinch salt

Process all of the ingredients together until evenly combined.
Using a small ice-cream scoop, shape the mixture into 10 or so balls.
Place them on the tray of a dehydrator, if you have one, and let dry
for 6 hours at 108°F (42°C). If you do not have a dehydrator,
chill the macarons overnight in the refrigerator.

power snack

. . . .

Makes about 9 oz. (250 g)
___

3½ tbsp (70 g) maple syrup
1½ tbsp (10 g) unsweetened cocoa
   powder

1 tsp powdered maca root
1 pinch chili powder
1½ cups (7½ oz./210 g) cashews

Preheat the oven to 300°F (150°C/Gas mark 2). Line a baking sheet
with parchment paper. Heat the maple syrup gently in a small saucepan
until bubbling and then stir in the cocoa powder, maca root powder,
and chili powder. Mix well and then remove from the heat. Add the cashews,
stirring until they are coated in the syrup. Tip out of the saucepan onto
the baking sheet, spread out evenly, and bake for 30 minutes. Remove
from the oven and let cool for 10 minutes. Break into pieces and store
in an airtight container.

wild bounty bites

Makes about 10

—

1 cup (3 oz./80 g) unsweetened shredded coconut,
  plus extra for sprinkling
2 tbsp (25 g) coconut oil
1½ tbsp (25 g) maple syrup
½ tsp ground vanilla bean
1 pinch salt
1 tsp water
1 oz. (25 g) vegan dark chocolate

 Line a baking sheet with parchment paper. In a mixing bowl, combine all of the ingredients, apart from the chocolate.

 Using a small ice-cream scoop, shape the mixture into 10 or so balls, releasing them onto the lined baking sheet. Chill for at least 1 hour.

 Melt the chocolate and dip the balls in it until coated. Sprinkle with shredded coconut and chill in the refrigerator until ready to serve.

love bars

Makes 10

1½ cups (9 oz./250 g) almonds
7 oz. (200 g) date paste
1 tsp coconut oil
1 pinch ground vanilla bean
1½ tbsp (10 g) cocoa nibs

2 tbsp (15 g) unsweetened cocoa powder, plus extra for dusting
1 tsp powdered maca root
2 tsp cocoa butter
1 tbsp (4 g) guarana powder
1 pinch salt

Line a baking sheet with parchment paper. Roughly chop the almonds and process them with the remaining ingredients to make a paste. Spread the paste over the lined sheet, pressing it down into an even layer, about ½ in. (1 cm) thick. Chill for at least 2 hours until firm, then cut into 10 bars. Return the bars to the refrigerator. Keep chilled until ready to serve. Dust with cocoa powder just before serving.

spirulina popcorn

Makes 7 oz. (200 g)

----

7 oz. (200 g) popcorn kernels
1 tbsp plus 2 tsp (20 g) coconut oil
1 tsp Himalayan salt
1 tbsp (7 g) spirulina powder

Using a popcorn popper or large saucepan, pop the corn with the coconut oil, ensuring you cover the saucepan with a lid. When the kernels have finished popping, add the salt and spirulina. Mix well and serve.

matcha bars

Makes 10

1 cup (5 oz./150 g) cashews
Generous ¾ cup (4½ oz./120 g) almonds
10 oz. (280 g) date paste
1 tsp ground vanilla bean
1 tbsp (6 g) matcha green tea powder, plus extra for sprinkling
⅔ cup (1¾ oz./50 g) unsweetened shredded coconut
1 pinch salt

1 Line a baking sheet with parchment paper. Roughly chop the cashews and almonds and process them with the rest of the ingredients to make a paste.

2 Spread the paste over the lined sheet, pressing it down into an even layer, about ½ in. (1 cm) thick. Chill for at least 2 hours.

3 Once the mixture is firm, cut into 10 bars. Return the bars to the refrigerator. Keep chilled until ready to serve. Sprinkle with matcha powder just before serving.

#drinks

. . . .

At Wild & the Moon, we like to drink, which is a good thing as we all need to stay hydrated. What's more, our drinks are energy-boosting, make your skin glow, boost your immunity, deep-cleanse your systems, and help deal with the stresses of everyday life. Are our juices magical? The truth lies at the bottom of the cup.

bam shot

Makes 1 shot (¼ cup/60 ml)

———

½-in. (1-cm) piece fresh ginger
⅓ oz. (10 g) fresh turmeric
Juice of ½ lemon
A drizzle of coconut oil
1 pinch freshly ground black pepper

Peel and pass the ginger and turmeric through a cold press juicer with the other ingredients.
Chill until ready to drink.

Health benefits
Anti-inflammatory

beauty shot

Makes 1 shot (¼ cup/60 ml)

———

2 oz. (50 g) fresh pomegranate seeds
1 tbsp (6 g) acai berry powder
¾-in. (2-cm) piece aloe vera leaf, washed
1 tbsp (15 ml) lemon juice
1 tsp sumac
A few goji berries

Pass all the ingredients through a cold press juicer.
Chill until ready to drink.

Health benefits
Rich in antioxidants

beach body

Makes 4 cups (1 liter)

—

1 watermelon
10 mint leaves, washed

Cut off the outer green part of the watermelon rind (as it can be harsh on the stomach) and chop the pink flesh and white part of the rind into chunks. Pass the watermelon chunks and mint through a cold press juicer. Mix well and drink immediately.

Note: Citrulline, a compound found especially in the white rind that surrounds the watermelon flesh, expels free radicals. It is converted into amino acids, which protect the heart and prevent toxins remaining in the body.

better than botox

Makes 4 cups (1 liter)

—

2 oz. (50 g) aloe vera leaves
8 red-skinned apples, washed and cut into chunks
1 cucumber, washed and cut into chunks

1 small raw red beet, cut into chunks
2 oz. (50 g) pomegranate seeds
1 tbsp plus 1 tsp (20 ml) lemon juice

Remove the skin from the aloe vera leaves, keeping only the flesh, and rinse. Pass the apples, cucumber, beet, aloe vera, and pomegranate seeds through a cold press juicer. Stir in the lemon juice. Mix well and drink immediately.

Health benefits
Moisturizes and protects the skin
Rich in antioxidants

black lemonade

Makes 4 cups (1 liter)

———

3 cups (700 ml) water
2½ tbsp (50 g) maple syrup
1¼ cups (300 ml) lemon juice
1 tsp food grade activated charcoal powder
½ tsp cider vinegar

Stir all of the ingredients together until combined. Chill until ready to drink.

Health benefits
Cleanses the body
Very good the day after a party, or in the evening before going to bed for a
flat stomach the next morning

hibiscus iced tea

Makes 4 cups (1 liter)

———

4 cups (1 liter) water
2 yerba mate teabags
20 dried hibiscus flowers
1½ tbsp (30 g) maple syrup

Heat the water to 175°F (80°C), infuse the teabags in it for 15 minutes,
and then remove. Add the hibiscus flowers and maple syrup, and stir to mix.
Chill until ready to drink.

black gold

Makes 4 cups (1 liter)

———

3¾ cups (900 ml) almond mylk (recipe p. 218)
2 oz. (60 g) date paste
1 tsp food grade activated charcoal powder

Blend the almond mylk and date paste together, then stir in the charcoal powder. Drink immediately.

Health benefits
Cleanses the body
Aids digestion

blue star

. . . .

Makes 2 cups (500 ml)

———

1⅔ cups (400 ml) unpasteurized coconut water
⅓ cup (90 ml) coconut milk
1 tsp blue spirulina powder
1 tsp reishi mushroom powder
1 tsp ground cinnamon
1 whole star anise

Stir all the ingredients together. Leave to infuse for 2 hours and then remove
the star anise. Chill until ready to drink.

Health benefits
Aids digestion
Stimulates the immune system

coffee chaga mylk

. . . .

Makes 4 cups (1 liter)

———

1⅔ cups (400 ml) cold brew coffee
1¾ oz. (50 g) date paste
1 tsp chaga mushroom powder
2½ cups (600 ml) almond mylk (recipe p. 218)
1 tbsp (10 g) gluten-free oatmeal

Blend the coffee, date paste, and chaga powder together. Stir in the almond
mylk and the oatmeal. Chill until ready to drink.

Health benefits
A gentle way to wake up in the morning

matcha mylk

Makes 4 cups (1 liter)

———

3¾ cups (900 ml) almond mylk (recipe p. 218)
2 oz. (60 g) date paste, or 2 tbsp (40 g) maple syrup
1 tbsp (6 g) matcha green tea powder
1 tsp green spirulina powder

Blend the almond mylk and date paste or maple syrup together.
Stir in the matcha and spirulina powders. Chill until ready to drink.

Health benefits
Antioxidant
Energy booster

hollyweed

Makes 4 cups (1 liter)

———

3 tbsp (60 g) maple syrup
1 tsp CBD isolate powder
1 pinch ground vanilla bean
A drizzle of coconut oil
2 tsp orange blossom water
1 pinch salt
3¾ cups (900 ml) cashew mylk (recipe p. 218)

Stir the maple syrup, CBD isolate powder, vanilla, coconut oil, orange
blossom water, and salt into the cashew mylk, mixing well.
Chill until ready to drink.

Health benefits
Anti-stress
Relaxant

la vie en rose

. . . .

Makes 4 cups (1 liter)

———

Scant 4 cups (940 ml) barista mylk (recipe p. 220)
2 tbsp (40 g) maple syrup
1 tbsp plus 1 tsp (20 ml) rose water
2 tsp beet juice
1 oz. (30 g) chia seeds

Combine all of the ingredients and chill until ready to drink.

Health benefits
Antibacterial and hydrating
Deep-cleanses the skin from the inside out

golden mylk

. . . .

Makes 4 cups (1 liter)

———

3¾ cups (900 ml) almond mylk
  (recipe p. 218)
2 oz. (60 g) date paste
1 tsp ground turmeric
1 tsp ground cinnamon

Juice from a ¾-in. (2-cm) piece
  of fresh ginger
1 tsp ground vanilla bean
1 tsp freshly ground black pepper
1 whole clove
1 pinch Himalayan salt

Blend together the almond mylk, date paste, spices, and salt.
Chill until ready to drink.

Health benefits
Powerful anti-inflammatory

keep it clean

Makes about 4 cups (1 liter)

———

3 oz. (80 g) celery stalk, washed and cut into chunks
3 oz. (80 g) cucumber, washed and cut into chunks
½-in. (1-cm) piece fresh ginger, washed
1½ oz. (40 g) spinach leaves, washed thoroughly
2 tbsp plus 2 tsp (40 ml) lemon juice

Pass the celery and cucumber through a cold press juicer, followed by the ginger and spinach. Add the lemon juice, stir well, and drink immediately.

Health benefits
Antioxidant
High in fiber
Aids digestion

down to earth

Makes about 4 cups (1 liter)

———

½-in. (1-cm) piece fresh ginger, washed
10 carrots, washed
6 small pears, preferably Williams or Bartlett, washed
⅓ cup (80 ml) lemon juice
1 pinch ground cinnamon

Pass the ginger, carrots, and pears through a cold press juicer.
Stir in the lemon juice and cinnamon. Mix well and drink immediately.

Health benefits
Invigorating / Helps purify the blood
Detoxifies the liver / Anti-inflammatory

kiwimandjaro

Makes about 4 cups (1 liter)

———

1 small pineapple, peeled and cut into chunks
1 kiwi, peeled and cut into chunks

3½ oz. (100 g) spinach leaves, washed thoroughly
1 tsp baobab powder
1 tsp moringa powder

Pass the pineapple, kiwi, and spinach through a cold press juicer and stir in the baobab and moringa powders. Mix well and drink immediately.

Health benefits
Rich in vitamin C, antioxidants, and calcium
Energy booster

little miss sunshine

Makes about 4 cups (1 liter)

———

1 pineapple, peeled and cut into chunks
1 cucumber, washed and cut into chunks
½-in. (1-cm) piece fresh ginger, washed
2 tsp ground turmeric
A few basil leaves, washed
1 tsp freshly ground black pepper

Pass the pineapple, cucumber, and ginger through a cold press juicer and stir in the turmeric, basil, and pepper. Mix well and drink immediately.

Health benefits
Rich in vitamin C
Energy booster

simply green

· ·

Makes about 4 cups (1 liter)

——

1 large cucumber, washed and cut into chunks
4 red-skinned apples, washed and cut into chunks
1 large bulb fennel, washed and cut into chunks
3½ oz. (100 g) kale or spinach leaves, washed thoroughly
1 tbsp plus 1 tsp (20 ml) lemon juice
1 tsp green spirulina powder

Pass the cucumber, apples, fennel, and kale or spinach through a cold press juicer. Stir in the lemon juice and spirulina powder. Mix well and drink immediately.

Health benefits
Detoxifying
Rich in vegetable proteins

sexy red

· ·

Makes about 4 cups (1 liter)

——

1 red bell pepper, washed, halved, and seeded
3½ oz. (100 g) strawberries, washed
8 red-skinned apples, washed and cut into chunks
2 tbsp (30 ml) lemon juice
½ tsp Cayenne pepper

Pass the pepper, strawberries, and apples through a cold press juicer and stir in the lemon juice and Cayenne pepper. Mix well and drink immediately.

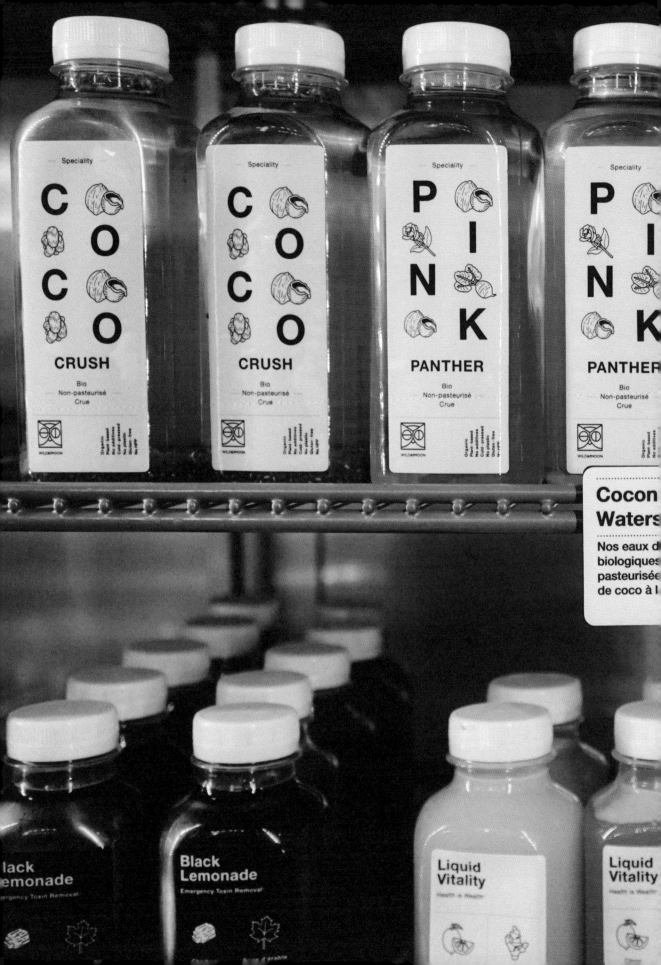

moon river

· ·

Makes about 4 cups (1 liter)

———

4 large pomelos, peeled and cut into chunks
7 small pears, washed and cut into chunks
1 tbsp (5 g) dried culinary lavender
1 tsp powdered maca root

Pass the pomelos and pears through a cold press juicer.
Stir in the lavender and maca powder. Mix well and drink immediately.

lucky five

· ·

Makes about 4 cups (1 liter)

———

6 oz. (160 g) raw red beet, peeled and cut into chunks
6 red-skinned apples, washed and cut into chunks
4 carrots, washed and cut into chunks
2 tsp ginger juice
2 tsp ground cinnamon
1 tbsp plus 1 tsp (20 ml) lemon juice

Pass the beet, apples, and carrots through a cold press juicer.
Stir in the ginger juice, cinnamon, and lemon juice.
Mix well and drink immediately.

Health benefits
Rich in calcium, iron, beta carotene, and antioxidants
Boosts the immune system

#at the bar

....

Yellow, green, blue, black, or pink: whatever the color,
I love plant-based lattes, hot or cold, at any time of the day.
They're a comfort food to be enjoyed to your heart's content.
Lattes, bowls, porridge, and smoothies—every taste brings
you a step closer to relaxation and well-being. Here's
a selection of all-day pick-me-ups served at the Wild counter.

lattes
chai latte 190 **matcha latte** 190 **golden latte** 191
charcoal latte 191 **chocolate chaga** 192 **coffee latte** 192
smurf latte 194 **rose latte** 194 **maca mug** 195
amazake 195

energy bowls/porridge
acai bowl 196 **matcha bowl** 196 **dragon bowl** 199
wild budwig 200 **blue majik bowl** 200 **cosmic bowl** 202
moon porridge 205

smoothies
kid smoothie 206 **chia matcha** 206 **blue moon** 208
ocean dream 208 **monkey mylk** 210 **protein shake** 213
namaste 214 **smooth green** 214

chai latte

Serves 1

——

½ tsp chai spice mix
1 tbsp (20 g) maple syrup
1 cup (250 ml) barista mylk (recipe p. 220)
To serve:
Ground cinnamon

Mix the chai spices and maple syrup with 1 tbsp (15 ml) hot water. Heat the barista mylk to the desired temperature and stir in the spiced water. Mix well and pour into a large cup. Dust with ground cinnamon and drink hot.

Health benefits
Rich in antioxidants / Anti-inflammatory
The ultimate comfort drink, to be enjoyed throughout the day

matcha latte

Serves 1

——

½ tsp matcha green tea powder
1 tbsp (20 g) maple syrup
1 cup (250 ml) barista mylk (recipe p. 220)
To serve:
Green spirulina powder

Stir the matcha powder and maple syrup into 1 tbsp (15 ml) hot water. Heat the barista mylk to the desired temperature and stir in the matcha and maple syrup water until combined. Pour into a large cup, sprinkle with spirulina powder, and drink hot.

Health benefits
Antioxidant / Energy booster / Rich in proteins

golden latte

· ·

Serves 1

——

½ tsp chai spice mix
½ tsp ground turmeric
1 tbsp (20 g) maple syrup
1 cup (250 ml) barista mylk
  (recipe p. 220)

To serve:
Freshly ground black pepper
Cayenne pepper

Mix the chai spices, turmeric, and maple syrup with 1 tbsp (15 ml) hot water.
Heat the barista mylk to the desired temperature and stir in the spice
and maple syrup water. Mix well and pour into a large cup.
Sprinkle with black pepper and Cayenne pepper and drink hot.

Health benefits
Powerful anti-inflammatory

charcoal latte

· ·

Serves 1

——

½ tsp food grade activated
  charcoal powder
1 tsp rice bran
1 tbsp (20 g) maple syrup

1 cup (250 ml) barista mylk
  (recipe p. 220)
To serve:
Food grade activated charcoal powder

Mix the charcoal powder, rice bran, and maple syrup with 1 tbsp (15 ml)
hot water. Heat the barista mylk to the desired temperature and stir
in the charcoal powder mixture until combined. Pour into a large cup,
sprinkle with charcoal powder, and drink hot.

Health benefits
Aids digestion / Contributes to glowing skin and healthy hair and nails
(thanks to the rice bran) / Helps prevent bloating

chocolate chaga

· ·

Serves 1

————

1 tbsp (7 g) unsweetened cocoa powder
1 tsp chaga powder
1 tbsp (20 g) maple syrup
1 cup (250 ml) barista mylk (recipe p. 220)
To serve:
Unsweetened cocoa powder

Stir the cocoa powder, chaga powder, and maple syrup into 1 tbsp (15 ml) hot water. Heat the barista mylk to the desired temperature and stir in the cocoa powder mixture. When combined, pour into a large cup. Dust with cocoa powder and drink hot.

Health benefits
Natural anti-depressant
Boosts metabolism and the immune system

coffee latte

· ·

Serves 1

————

1 cup (250 ml) barista mylk (recipe p. 220)
2 shots espresso

Heat the barista mylk to the desired temperature and stir in the espresso shots. Pour into a large cup and drink hot.

Health benefits
Fights fatigue

smurf latte

. . . .

Serves 1

———

1 cup (250 ml) barista mylk
  (recipe p. 220)
1 tsp blue spirulina powder
1 tsp rice bran
1 tbsp (20 g) maple syrup

To serve:
Blue spirulina powder

Heat the barista mylk with the spirulina, rice bran, and maple syrup
to the desired temperature. Pour into a large cup, sprinkle with blue spirulina
powder, and drink hot.

Health benefits
Rich in iron and vegetable proteins

rose latte

. . . .

Serves 1

———

1 tsp beet juice
1 tsp rose water
1 tbsp (20 g) maple syrup
1 cup (250 ml) barista mylk
  (recipe p. 220)

To serve:
Red beet powder

Mix the beet juice, rose water, and maple syrup together.
Heat the barista mylk to the desired temperature and pour the beet juice
mixture into it. Stir well and pour into a large cup. Sprinkle with the beet
powder and drink hot.

Health benefits
For a fresh complexion

maca mug

Serves 1

———

1 tsp powdered maca root
1 tbsp (20 g) maple syrup
1 cup (250 ml) barista mylk
  (recipe p. 220)

To serve:
Ground cinnamon

Mix the maca root and maple syrup with 1 tbsp (15 ml) hot water.
Heat the barista mylk to the desired temperature and add the maca root
mixture. Stir well and pour into a large cup. Sprinkle with cinnamon
and drink hot.

Health benefits
Aphrodisiac

amazake

Serves 1

———

1 cup (250 ml) almond mylk
  (recipe p. 218)
2 tsp amazake
1 pinch ground cardamom
1 pinch coconut sugar

To serve:
Ground cardamom

Heat the almond mylk to the desired temperature and then stir in the amazake,
cardamom, and coconut sugar. Stir well and pour into a large cup.
Sprinkle with extra cardamom and drink hot.

Health benefits
Boosts the production of melanin. Perfect for lovely skin.

acai bowl

· ·

Serves 1
——

1 banana, peeled
2 tsp frozen unsweetened acai berries
1 tbsp (15 ml) almond mylk
   (recipe p. 218)
1 tbsp (20 g) maple syrup

To serve:
2 oz. (50 g) granola of your choice
Banana slices or seasonal fruits
Shredded coconut

Blend all the ingredients together until smooth and creamy.
Serve accompanied by the granola, banana slices or seasonal fruits,
and sprinkle with shredded coconut.

Health benefits
Rich in antioxidants

matcha bowl

· ·

Serves 1
——

1 banana, peeled, sliced, and frozen
2 tsp matcha green tea powder
1 tsp green spirulina powder
4 tbsp (60 ml) almond mylk
   (recipe p. 218)

To serve:
2 slices kiwi fruit
Unsweetened coconut flakes
Blueberries
1 tsp hemp seeds

Blend all the ingredients together until smooth and creamy.
Serve accompanied by the kiwi slices, coconut flakes, blueberries,
and hemp seeds.

Health benefits
Boosts the immune system
Rich in antioxidants

dragon bowl

Serves 1
———

3½ oz. (100 g) dragon fruit (pitaya) flesh, frozen
1 banana, peeled
2 oz. (50 g) frozen strawberries
2 tbsp (30 ml) coconut milk
To serve:
Granola of your choice
1 tsp cranberries
1 slice kiwi fruit

Blend all the ingredients together until smooth and creamy.
Serve accompanied by the granola, cranberries, and a slice of kiwi fruit.

Health benefits
Rich in fiber and antioxidants

wild budwig

. . . .

Serves 1

——

1 banana, peeled and sliced
1 handful sprouted almonds
½ apple, washed, cored, and roughly
   chopped
A few drops lemon juice
1 pinch green spirulina powder
1 tsp linseed (flaxseed) oil

1 tbsp (10 g) buckwheat or millet,
   freshly ground
To serve:
Seasonal fruits
A few walnuts or almonds,
   roughly chopped
1 pinch green spirulina powder

Blend all the ingredients together until smooth and creamy.
Serve accompanied by the seasonal fruits, and sprinkle
over the chopped walnuts or almonds and spirulina powder.

Health benefits
Rich in essential fatty acids
The ideal breakfast

blue majik bowl

. . . .

Serves 1

——

1 banana, peeled
3 oz. (75 g) frozen pineapple pieces
1 tsp blue spirulina powder
2 tbsp (30 ml) coconut milk

To serve:
2 oz. (50 g) granola of your choice
2 tbsp (25 g) blueberries
1 slice kiwi fruit
1 tsp unsweetened shredded coconut
1 pinch blue spirulina powder

Blend all the ingredients together until smooth and creamy.
Serve accompanied by the granola, blueberries, and kiwi slice,
and sprinkle with shredded coconut and blue spirulina powder.

cosmic bowl

··

Serves 1

———

1 banana, peeled, sliced, and frozen
1 tsp food grade activated charcoal powder
1 tsp fennel seeds
1 tsp ground vanilla bean
4 tbsp (60 ml) almond mylk (recipe p. 218)
To serve:
Granola of your choice
Fresh blueberries, washed

Blend all the ingredients together until smooth and creamy.
Serve accompanied by the granola and blueberries.

Health benefits
Absorbs toxins
Aids digestion

moon porridge

Serves 1

------

2 cups (500 ml) almond mylk (recipe p. 218) or coconut milk
1¾ oz. (50 g) gluten-free rolled oats
A few raisins, soaked to rehydrate them
A drizzle of maple syrup
1 pinch ground cinnamon
To serve:
Banana slices
Chopped red-skinned apple
1 tbsp (15 g) almond butter

For hot porridge: heat the almond mylk or coconut milk in a saucepan. When it is hot, add the oats in a thin stream, stirring until combined. Add the raisins, maple syrup, and cinnamon and set aside for about 10 minutes, stirring from time to time.

For cold porridge: let the oats and other ingredients soak overnight in the almond mylk or coconut milk.

Serve the porridge hot or cold, accompanied by banana slices, chopped apple, and almond butter.

Health benefits
A healthy breakfast for all the family

kid smoothie

· ·

Serves 1

———

1 banana, peeled
About 3 frozen strawberries
1 tbsp (20 g) maple syrup
1⅔ cups (400 ml) almond mylk (recipe p. 218)

Blend all the ingredients together to make a fairly thick smoothie.

Health benefits
Energy booster
Great for children or adults who enjoy simple flavors

chia matcha

· ·

Serves 1

———

1 banana, peeled, sliced, and frozen
2 tsp matcha green tea powder
1 tbsp (10 g) chia seeds
2 tsp coconut or almond butter
1 tbsp (20 g) maple syrup
1 pinch ground vanilla bean
1⅔ cups (400 ml) almond mylk (recipe p. 218)

Blend all the ingredients together to make a fairly thick smoothie.

Health benefits
Energy booster
Aids digestion
Perfect for sporty types
Rich in protein

blue moon

· ·

Serves 1

———

1 banana, peeled
4½ oz. (125 g) frozen blueberries
1 kale leaf, washed
1 tsp powdered maca root
1 tbsp (20 g) maple syrup
1⅔ cups (400 ml) almond mylk (recipe p. 218)

Blend all the ingredients together to make a fairly thick smoothie.

Health benefits
Boosts metabolism and the immune system / Antioxidant
Helps make your skin glow (thanks to the blueberries and kale)

ocean dream

· ·

Serves 1

———

1 banana, peeled, sliced, and frozen
2 tsp blue spirulina powder
1 probiotic sachet
1 tsp rice bran
1 tbsp (20 g) maple syrup
1 pinch ground vanilla bean
1⅔ cups (400 ml) coconut milk

Blend all the ingredients together to make a fairly thick smoothie.

Health benefits
Good for intestinal flora
Rich in vitamin B12

monkey mylk

Serves 1

———

1 banana, peeled, sliced, and frozen
1 tbsp (7 g) unsweetened cocoa powder
1 tsp green spirulina powder
1 tbsp (15 g) almond butter
1 pinch ground vanilla bean
1 tbsp (20 g) maple syrup
1⅔ cups (400 ml) almond mylk (recipe p. 218)

Blend all the ingredients together to make a fairly thick smoothie.

Health benefits
Detoxifying
Excellent for keeping your spirits up

protein shake

Serves 1
----

1 banana, peeled, sliced, and frozen
1 tbsp (15 g) vanilla vegan protein powder
1 tbsp (10 g) hemp seeds
1 tbsp (15 ml) orange blossom water
½ tbsp (7 g) almond butter
1⅔ cups (400 ml) almond mylk (recipe p. 218)

Blend all the ingredients together to make a fairly thick smoothie.

Health benefits
Perfect for sporty types
Helps tone up muscles

namaste

· ·

Serves 1

——

1 banana, peeled
2 oz. (50 g) dragon fruit (pitaya) flesh, frozen
1 tsp mixed relaxing adaptogenic mushrooms,
  such as ashwaganda, reishi, and chaga
1 tbsp (20 g) maple syrup
1⅔ cups (400 ml) almond mylk (recipe p. 218)

Blend all the ingredients together to make a fairly thick smoothie.

Health benefits
Relaxant
Highly concentrated source of fiber and vitamin C
Antioxidant

smooth green

· ·

Serves 1

——

1 banana, peeled, sliced, and frozen
½ green-skinned apple, washed
1 kale leaf, washed
1 pinch ground vanilla bean
1 tsp green spirulina powder

4 drops lemon juice
½ tsp hemp seeds
1⅔ cups (400 ml) unpasteurized
  coconut water

Blend all the ingredients together to make a fairly thick smoothie.

Health benefits
Good for the heart
Helps make your skin glow
Super-hydrating

#basic recipes

· ·

It's often said that the simplest things in life are the best,
but whether we're talking food or fashion, it's important
to get the basics right. Neo-Chantilly whipped cream;
cashew, almond, and hemp mylks; miso mayonnaise; or
spirulina sauce: these essentials can make all the difference.
Here's the proof, with 14 building-block recipes.

almond mylk

Makes 4 cups (1 liter)

———

1 cup (5 oz./150 g) almonds
4 cups (1 liter) water,
    preferably filtered

1 pinch ground vanilla bean
1 pinch salt
1 tsp coconut oil (optional)

Soak the almonds in a bowl of cold water in the refrigerator for 12 hours or overnight. Drain and rinse well. Transfer the almonds to a blender, add the 4 cups (1 liter) water and blend well (do this in batches, if necessary). Strain through a nut milk bag or fine cheesecloth, pressing down well on the almond pulp. Strain the liquid through a fine-mesh sieve, reserving the almond pulp for another recipe. Add the vanilla, salt, and coconut oil (if using), mixing well. Pour into a bottle or other container. The mylk can be stored for up to 3 days in the refrigerator.

cashew mylk

Makes 4 cups (1 liter)

———

1 cup (5 oz./150 g) cashews
4 cups (1 liter) water, preferably filtered
1 pinch ground vanilla bean
1 pinch salt
1 tsp coconut oil (optional)

Soak the cashews in a bowl of cold water for 8 hours. Drain and rinse well. Transfer the cashews to a blender, add the 4 cups (1 liter) water and blend well (do this in batches, if necessary). Strain through a nut milk bag or fine cheesecloth, pressing down well. Strain the cashew mylk through a fine-mesh sieve and add the vanilla, salt, and coconut oil (if using), mixing well. Pour into a bottle or other container. The mylk can be stored for up to 3 days in the refrigerator.

barista mylk

Makes generous 4 cups (1 liter)

————

3¾ cups (900 ml) almond mylk (recipe p. 218)
Scant ½ cup (100 ml) coconut milk

Mix the two milks together until combined. Pour into a bottle or other container. The mylk can be stored for up to 3 days in the refrigerator.

hemp mylk

Makes scant 3¼ cups (750 ml)

————

Scant 1 cup (5 oz./150 g) hulled hemp seeds
3¼ cups (750 ml) water, preferably filtered
1 tbsp (20 g) maple syrup
1 pinch ground vanilla bean

Soak the hemp seeds in a bowl of cold water overnight. Drain and rinse well. Transfer the seeds to a blender, add the 3¼ cups (750 ml) water, maple syrup, and ground vanilla, and blend at high speed for 1 minute. Strain through a nut milk bag or fine cheesecloth and pour into a bottle or other container. The mylk can be stored for up to 3 days in the refrigerator.

vanilla cream

· ·

Makes about 8 oz. (225 g)

———

⅔ cup (3½ oz./100 g) cashews
2 tbsp (40 g) maple syrup
1 pinch ground vanilla bean
¼ cup (60 ml) water

Soak the cashews in a bowl of cold water for 8 hours, then drain and rinse well. Process or blend them with the remaining ingredients until smooth and creamy.

wild chantilly cream

· ·

Makes about 1 lb. (500 g)

———

Scant ½ cup (100 ml) cashew mylk (recipe p. 218)
1 cup (240 ml) coconut milk
3 tbsp (60 g) maple syrup
1 pinch ground vanilla bean

Chill a siphon and all the ingredients in the refrigerator for 2 hours before making the recipe. Mix the chilled ingredients together until thoroughly combined and transfer to the siphon. Return the siphon to the refrigerator until ready to serve the cream. To serve, press down on the siphon lever to dispense the cream.

Note: Before using the whipping siphon, it is important to read
the manufacturer's instructions and follow them carefully.
Make sure you do not overfill the siphon, as this is potentially dangerous.

pico de gallo

Makes scant ½ cup (3½ oz./100 g)

———

1 avocado, pitted, peeled, and flesh finely diced
1 ripe tomato, washed and finely diced
½ red onion, peeled and finely chopped
A few cilantro leaves, washed and finely chopped
1 tsp mild chili powder
1 tsp paprika flakes
3 tbsp (45 ml) olive oil
1 tbsp (15 ml) lemon juice
Salt and pepper

In a bowl, mix together the diced avocado and tomato with the onion and cilantro. Stir in the chili powder, paprika flakes, olive oil, and lemon juice. Season with salt and pepper.

bò bún sauce

Makes scant ½ cup (100 ml)

———

3 tbsp (60 g) maple syrup
1 tsp fresh ginger juice
1 garlic clove, peeled and crushed
  (leave whole if you prefer to remove before serving)
3 tbsp (45 ml) tamari
3 tbsp (45 ml) rice vinegar

Heat the maple syrup in a small saucepan (or in a bowl in the microwave) with the ginger juice and garlic. As soon as the mixture bubbles, remove from the heat and add the tamari and rice vinegar. You can remove the garlic just before serving, if you wish.

spirulina sauce

Makes about ⅔ cup (5 oz./150 g)

---

1 large handful cashews
1 tbsp (15 ml) cider vinegar
1 tbsp (15 ml) mustard
3 tbsp (45 ml) olive oil
1 tsp green spirulina powder
2 tbsp (30 ml) water
Salt

Soak the cashews in a bowl of cold water for 8 hours. Drain, rinse well, and blend with the other ingredients until smooth and creamy.

citrus vinaigrette

Makes about ½ cup (120 ml)

---

1 leek, white part only, cut into 4 pieces
¼-in. (½-cm) piece fresh ginger, peeled and roughly chopped
6 tbsp (90 ml) olive oil
1 tbsp (15 ml) lemon juice
1 tbsp (15 ml) orange juice
1 pinch salt

Gently heat the leek and ginger in the olive oil. Remove from the heat and leave overnight to infuse. Remove the leek. Put the lemon and orange juices and salt in a deep bowl and whisk in the infused olive oil in a thin drizzle until a smooth emulsion is obtained.

white cashew sauce

Makes about 1 cup (8 oz./225 g)

____

Generous ½ cup (2½ oz./70 g)
  cashews
2 tbsp (30 ml) lemon juice
4 tbsp (60 ml) olive oil
2 tbsp (30 ml) sesame oil
1 tsp tamari
1 tbsp (15 ml) fresh ginger juice
3 tbsp (45 ml) water
Salt and pepper

To serve:
Finely chopped onion, chopped
  chives, paprika, green spirulina
  powder, or chopped garlic

Soak the cashews in a bowl of cold water for 8 hours. Drain, rinse well,
and blend with the other ingredients until smooth and creamy.
Season with salt and pepper. You can flavor the sauce with onion,
chives, paprika, spirulina, or garlic.

miso mayonnaise

Makes scant 1 cup (7 oz./200 g)

____

⅓ cup (2 oz./50 g) cashews
¼ garlic clove, peeled and crushed
2 tbsp (30 ml) lemon juice
1 tbsp (15 ml) umeboshi (ume plum)
  vinegar

1½ tbsp (25 ml) cider vinegar
1½ tbsp (25 ml) olive oil
2 oz. (50 g) white miso paste
4 tbsp (60 ml) water
Salt and pepper

Soak the cashews in a bowl of cold water for 8 hours, then drain and rinse
well. Blend all the ingredients together until smooth and creamy.

basil pesto

Makes about 9 oz. (250 g)

——

1 bunch basil leaves, washed
½ bunch flat-leaf parsley, washed
2 oz. (50 g) pine nuts or hazelnuts, toasted
1 large or 2 small garlic cloves, peeled and chopped
⅔ cup (150 ml) olive oil
Salt and pepper

Blend all the ingredients together until smooth, adjusting the seasoning if necessary.

wild vegan cream cheese

Makes about 9 oz. (250 g)

——

1½ cups (7 oz./200 g) cashews
3 tbsp (45 ml) lemon juice
A few chive stems, washed and finely chopped
Salt and pepper

Soak the cashews in a bowl of cold water for 8 hours until softened. Drain, rinse well, and transfer to a blender. Add the lemon juice, season with salt and pepper, and blend until smooth and creamy. Store in the refrigerator. When ready to serve, lightly stir in the chives.
Serve accompanied by crackers or raw vegetable sticks.

#superfoods

....

What if some foods could truly change our lives?
If, by including them in our diet, we could all feel
so much better? Does that sound impossible?
Well, it's true. I'm referring to the famous superfoods
that have been used in the ancient traditions of many
cultures around the world for centuries.
Here, Wild & the Moon presents a selection
of the finest among them, to be discovered
(or re-discovered) without delay.

Let food be thy medicine and medicine be thy food.

—Hippocrates

Ingrédients

...use source
de vitamines
...ux essentiels
...mer sans
...on dans une
...tiède

Wild Tips

Brazil in a Ber

Wild Tips

...oab

Arbre Immortel

70 g

Wild Tips

Petit fruit au goût
acidulé, le baobab
est un tonique
général. En cure
contre l'état de
fatigue !

SUPERFOODS: THE MYSTERIES REVEALED

SUPERFOODS ARE A SPECIAL GROUP OF INGREDIENTS THAT ARE NATURE'S GIFT TO US. THERE'S NO SINGLE DEFINITION THAT COVERS THEM ALL BUT IT IS GENERALLY AGREED THAT SUPERFOODS ARE FRUIT, VEGETABLES, SEAWEED, HERBS, AND PLANTS THAT PROVIDE A MULTITUDE OF HEALTH BENEFITS AND HAVE A POSITIVE EFFECT ON OUR WELL-BEING. HIGHLY NUTRITIOUS AND NATURALLY GOOD FOR US, THEY ARE RICH IN VITAMINS, MINERALS, ANTIOXIDANTS, FIBERS, AND OTHER ESSENTIAL ELEMENTS. THEY'RE THE NEW MUST-EATS, SO GET TO KNOW THEM!

ACAI

ORIGIN — South America.

LOOK — Small purple berry, similar in appearance to a blueberry.

BENEFITS — Very rich in antioxidants, vitamins, and minerals. Acai berries protect the skin, help to prevent it aging, and may potentially reduce the risks of cardiovascular disease and some types of cancer.

BACKGROUND — There once was a young Amazonian woman named Iaca. Her father was the chief of a tribe whose population had grown so large that he could no longer feed all his people, and he decreed that all newborns should be killed. Soon after, Iaca gave birth to a child who was immediately put to death. The poor young woman wept for days, until one evening she heard a child crying and went in search of it. She found instead a palm tree laden with fruit and in despair she lay down under it, where she died of sorrow. The next day, the tribe found her body beneath the new tree and they ate its fruit, which left them replete and full of energy once again. Iaca's father revoked his cruel decree and the tribe prospered and grew. The tree was named after the chief's daughter: Iaca, when read backwards, is "acai."

USES — Blend frozen acai as your base in a smoothie or super bowl. In powder form, you can add it to all your snacks, smoothies, juices, and breakfast foods.

WILD TIPS — Add 1 tbsp of ground acai to whatever you're making, adjusting the quantity to suit your personal taste.

ACEROLA

ORIGIN — Amazonia.

LOOK — Small, bright red berry with orange-colored flesh.

BENEFITS — Anti-inflammatory, antioxidant, mega-rich in vitamin C (a single berry contains 30 to 40 times more vitamin C than an orange). Acerola is invigorating and helps boost the immune system.

BACKGROUND — The name comes from the Spanish for "maple cherry" and the tree that bears it is known as "the tree of health." Acerola has been widely used in tropical countries to relieve certain types of diarrhea, dysentery, and liver problems.

USES — In winter, or if you feel feverish, take it as a supplement to combat fatigue, stress, or burnout.

WILD TIPS — As a short-term course of treatment, take 2 capsules a day (one in the morning and one later in the day); as a supplement to your daily diet, take 1 capsule a day.

ACTIVATED CHARCOAL POWDER

ORIGIN — United States, Japan, France.

LOOK — Black powder made from the calcination of softwood such as poplar, lime trees, trembling aspen, and willow.

BENEFITS —With its purifying properties, it is a great detoxifier, relieving stomach aches and general digestive problems.

BACKGROUND — Proof exists that activated charcoal powder has been used in medicine since the time of Hippocrates, around 400 BCE. The Egyptians used it to purify water from about 1500 BCE, so its benefits have been known for over 2000 years. In early twentieth-century America, it was reputed to ward off typhoid, cholera, smallpox, and "malignant fevers," and to alleviate gastrointestinal disorders. During the same period, French physicians injected it intravenously—with some success— to combat tuberculosis. In the 1970s, it started being used as an antidote to poisons. It is even effective on insect bites and is recommended for people endeavoring to stop smoking, drinking, or taking drugs, as it absorbs the chemical substances that lead to addiction.

USES — Drop a stick of activated charcoal into your water jug, wait at least 3 hours, and lo and behold, your water will be purified!

WILD TIPS — Take 3 tsp, 30 minutes before lunch and dinner.

BAOBAB

ORIGIN — Tropical Africa.

LOOK — A mighty tree that can grow 65 feet (20 m) high, with a trunk up to 30 feet (10 m) in diameter. The flesh of its fruit is called "monkey bread."

BENEFITS — In Africa, every part of the tree—roots, leaves, trunk, bark, flesh, and seeds—is eaten for its healing and nutritional value. The "monkey bread" is especially rich in vitamins C (containing 7 times more than an orange), B, and A. With its calcium, potassium, iron, and manganese content, it's a good source of minerals, and also contains fibers, protein, and antioxidants.

BACKGROUND — This "magical tree," also called "pharmacy tree" or "tree of life," can live for hundreds of years.

USES — It's the perfect food to prevent malnutrition, particularly for the elderly, and is equally beneficial for pregnant women and infants.

WILD TIPS — Stir 1–3 tsp of baobab powder into your drinks or other recipes. It will add a sweet, tangy taste.

CBD OIL
ORIGIN — Asia.

LOOK — An oil extracted from the cannabis sativa plant, a member of the hemp family.

BENEFITS — Alleviates stomach aches and general digestive disorders.

BACKGROUND — Hemp, from which CBD derives, was one of the first plants to be cultivated by humans and has been used since 8000 BCE. CBD was isolated from it in 1939, at the University of Illinois, and in 1963 its calming and anti-inflammatory effects were demonstrate. CBD is recognized as being effective in relieving physical pain, such as headaches, muscular pains, and stomach cramps, and in reducing anxiety and stress.

USES — Our favorite remedy for a good night's sleep— you're guaranteed to wake up well rested and raring to go!

WILD TIPS — In oil form, take a few drops under your tongue. As a food supplement, take up to 8 tablets a day.

CHAGA
ORIGIN — Canada, Russia, Korea.

LOOK — A wild mushroom that grows on birch trees and is black on the outside and orange-brown on the inside.

BENEFITS — Chaga is the best antioxidant food there is and one of the most nutritious mushrooms in the world. It also helps the adrenal glands and digestive organs to function well.

BACKGROUND — The link between humans and chaga dates back to about 3500 BCE. In the Ötztal mountains, between Austria and Italy, a mummified body was found beneath a glacier. The mummy was named Otzi, and in the pouch found with the body were three varieties of mushroom, including chaga. The Khanty—reindeer herders in Siberia—brewed chaga as a tea to improve their digestion, and spread it on wounds to cleanse them. They even dried and smoked chaga to supposedly strengthen their lungs! For over 500 years now, it has been used for medicinal purposes in Russia, in particular in Siberia.

USES — In powder form, stir it into your coffee or smoothie, or drink as a warm or cold infusion in order to preserve its enzymes and vitamins (which are heat-sensitive).

WILD TIPS — Add 1 tsp chaga to a hot or cold drink once a day, as a supplement, or 2–3 times a day to boost your immune system.

CHAI
ORIGIN — Northern India.

LOOK — A mix of various spices, sometimes with black tea.

BENEFITS — Cloves, ginger, and cinnamon are well known for their anti-inflammatory properties and the antioxidants they contain help combat free radicals in the body and protect cells from stress. These spices are also known to improve digestion and help relieve stomach ache, which is one of the reasons why chai is generally drunk after meals.

BACKGROUND — It's redundant to talk of "chai tea" as "chai" literally means "tea." The countries it was shipped to usually referred to the drink as "tea," while those it was sent to overland called it "chai." Drinking chai is almost a religion in India where it is enjoyed hot and sweet at any time of the day.

USES — Drink it hot with homemade almond mylk and maple syrup, instead of cow's milk and refined sugar; in summer, try infusing it to make iced chai lattes.

WILD TIPS — 1–2 tsp in your favorite hot drink.

WE LOVE SUPERFOODS: THEY'RE THE BATMAN OF REGULAR FOOD.

CHIA
ORIGIN — Mexico.

LOOK — The chia plant is a member of the sage family and its seeds are small and often dark brown, although you can find lighter shades that are beige or grayish.

BENEFITS — Chia seeds are an antioxidant and rich in omega-3 and omega-6, so are an excellent source of fatty acids. They also contain vegetable proteins, vitamin B9, calcium, and magnesium. When soaked, chia seeds swell and a gelatinous substance forms around them that aids digestion and the better absorption of their nutritional benefits; however, even the dried seeds are digestible.

BACKGROUND — The Aztecs grew chia and were familiar with the numerous health benefits of the seeds, including sustaining physical energy (in the Mayan language "chia" means "strength") and intellectual focus. Chia was a staple food for many peoples of Central America, as a small quantity was sufficient to give them the stamina and endurance to keep fatigue at bay during their daily activities. Chia seeds were eaten roasted or ground and, after corn and beans, provided their third source of plant-based food.

USES — Make chia pudding, or add to cakes, mueslis, smoothies, and drinks.

WILD TIPS — To make two bowls of chia pudding, soak 4 heaping tbsp of chia seeds in 1⅔ cups (400 ml) of your favorite plant-based mylk.

CHLORELLA
ORIGIN — China.

LOOK — Green seaweed, which gets its color from the exceptionally large amount of chlorophyll it contains.

BENEFITS — Great for detoxification, extremely rich in chlorophyll, as well as vitamins, minerals, and oligo-elements. Its benefits are wide-ranging and it combines very well with other highly nutritious seaweeds and spirulina.

BACKGROUND — It has been around for 2 billion years.

USES — Take as a rehab shot: a combination of chlorella and spirulina that will thoroughly re-mineralize your body and cleanse and detoxify your entire organism. When extreme measures are called for—or to avoid needing them in the first place.

WILD TIPS — Take 1 tsp in a glass of water or fruit juice.

GINSENG
ORIGIN — China, Korea, and the far eastern regions of the former Soviet Union.

LOOK — A small perennial plant. Its roots are the part that is eaten.

BENEFITS — Helps fight fatigue, depression, and inflammation. It is an antioxidant, stimulates intellectual activity, protects the immune system, and is also a powerful aphrodisiac. In China and Korea, it is the number one superfood.

BACKGROUND — Ginseng's health-giving properties have been known in Asia for over 4,000 years when the plant was given to emperors and nobles as medication. Traditional Chinese doctors still claim that it can cure all ills. It has become the victim of its own success, so check the quality of the ginseng you are buying, as the rule of harvesting after 7 years of growth is no longer strictly adhered to.
USES — Make ginseng tea (popular in Korea), or add to soups, smoothies, and drinks.
WILD TIPS — 4 capsules per day, taken at regular intervals.

GUARANA

ORIGIN — The Amazonian rainforest.
LOOK — Small, bright red berries that open to reveal black-and-white flesh inside that resembles a staring eye.
BENEFITS — Guarana berries have become world famous because they contain guaranine, an invigorating substance that's 4 to 7 times more powerful than black coffee—minus the side effects. An ultra-healthy stimulant, the berry is energizing and invigorating. It boosts mental and physical reflexes, intellectual concentration, physical strength, and reduces fatigue. It also burns fat and is known to be an effective appetite suppressant.
BACKGROUND — The plant takes its name from the Guarani people who are indigenous to the Amazon and were the first to discover it. They ate it to combat fatigue and reduce their appetite during food shortages. In 1664, the missionary Father Felipe Bettendorf wrote, "It gives them so much strength that they can go hunting for two consecutive days without feeling any hunger. In addition, it alleviates fevers, cramps, and headaches."
USES — During periods when you're overworked, get into the habit of taking guarana every day.
WILD TIPS — Put 1 tsp in your favorite drink, preferably in the morning, before an exam or undertaking intense physical activity. With its high caffeine content, it's not advisable to add it to your coffee.

HEMP

ORIGIN — Central Asia.
LOOK — A plant that grows tall and straight with thin, palmate-shaped leaves.
BENEFITS — Hemp seeds are a good source of protein, minerals, vitamins, and fiber. They also have a balanced omega-3 and omega-6 content.
BACKGROUND — Hemp was one of the first plants to be domesticated by humans during the Neolithic period between 900 and 7000 BCE, most probably in Asia. It was carried on various migrations and conquests, and, as a result, spread to all parts of the world. Hemp and cannabis are varieties of the same plant species, but hemp seeds contain only a negligible amount of THC, the main psychoactive constituent of cannabis that gets you "high."
USES — With its hazelnut-like flavor, it is an excellent addition to both savory and sweet recipes. Add as an oil or seeds to salads, smoothies, and desserts.
WILD TIPS — Use 1 tbsp of oil in your vinaigrette, or sprinkle 1 tsp of seeds on your salads.

MACA

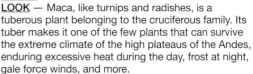

ORIGIN — Peru.
LOOK — Maca, like turnips and radishes, is a tuberous plant belonging to the cruciferous family. Its tuber makes it one of the few plants that can survive the extreme climate of the high plateaus of the Andes, enduring excessive heat during the day, frost at night, gale force winds, and more.
BENEFITS — Acknowledged as an aphrodisiac, maca is a tonic that invigorates and strengthens, as well as boosting the immune system generally. It is rich in vitamins, amino acids, essential fatty acids, minerals, and oligo-elements. Maca is an adaptogen, meaning it has a touch of magic, adapting to your body's needs in the same way as ginseng.
BACKGROUND — The Incas of the high plateaus of Peru always considered maca to be a sacred plant. They discovered it growing wild over 3,000 years ago at an altitude of 11,500 feet (3,500 m).
USES — Maca helps balance your hormonal system, so it's highly recommended for women experiencing difficulties adapting to a new contraceptive method or going through menopause. And it's *the* aphrodisiac par excellence!
WILD TIPS — Take a 3-week course of maca, adding a pinch to your favorite breakfast every morning.

MATCHA

ORIGIN — Japan.
LOOK — Fine green tea powder made by slowly grinding green tea leaves between two grinding stones. The leaves come from tea bushes that have been covered for 20–30 days prior to harvesting, to protect them from sunlight and increase the amount of chlorophyll in their leaves, which stimulates the production of amino acids.
BENEFITS — The powder dissolves in water and contains an enormous quantity of natural antioxidants that help combat free radicals, raised cholesterol, and keep the skin from aging. As the tea powder is ingested, rather than infused like tea made with leaves, it is an even richer source of substances such as caffeine and antioxidants, and its benefits are both stimulating and relaxing.
BACKGROUND — Zen Buddhist monks have been drinking matcha for over 800 years. At that time, the monks drank the tea mainly for medicinal purposes or as a stimulant to enable them to stay awake and concentrate fully during long hours of meditation. The practice was later adopted by the emperor of China and his court.
USES — Add to hot and cold drinks, smoothies, and energy bowls. It is delicious in desserts—an excellent compromise between a treat and a stimulant.
WILD TIPS — To make tea, infuse 1–2 tsp (about 2 g—to be adapted according to personal taste) per teapot, for an energy boost.

I THINK MY SOUL MATE MIGHT BE MATCHA

MORINGA

ORIGIN — Egypt.

LOOK — Moringa leaves are downy, bright green, and resemble fern leaves.

BENEFITS — With its high vitamin C content, it is one of the best superfoods for protecting against disease. The plant is a powerful antioxidant and a formidable ally if you want to slim, as it is rich in nutrients that help you lose weight. It also has chemical components that contribute to the regulation of blood sugar levels, so is useful in helping to lower cholesterol and prevent obesity.

BACKGROUND — Ancient Ayurvedic writings from India, dating back to 150 BCE, mention moringa and its use in the treatment of more than 300 diseases.

USES — Use moringa as you would matcha powder. It will give your desserts and other dishes a similar color, but it tastes less sweet.

WILD TIPS — To make tea, infuse 2–3 tsp per teapot, or stir into whatever you're cooking or drinking.

RAW CACAO

ORIGIN — Peru.

LOOK — The fresh cacao beans enclosed in the large, oval fruit (called a pod) look gluey because they are surrounded by a white pulp. Once dried, they turn dark brown and are an elongated oval shape.

BENEFITS — With their exceptional antioxidant powers, cacao beans are good for the heart (being rich in flavanols and other polyphenols) and very rich in potassium and other minerals.

BACKGROUND — Cacao has been known to humankind since about 2000 BCE, at the time of the Maya Empire. For the Maya, Toltec, and Bribrí peoples, cacao was a divine symbol that acted as a mediator between heaven and earth, and between nature and humankind. After the Spanish conquest, the cacao pod lost its symbolic value and became a form of currency. It is said to have been the origin of accounting in the Americas, where allegedly a rabbit could be bought for 10 beans and a slave for 100.

USES — Raw cacao is an excellent alternative to chocolate. The difference between raw cacao and the "classic" cocoa we are used to eating in our everyday chocolate is that the cacao beans have not been roasted.

WILD TIPS — Add to all your sweet recipes according to personal taste, but bear in mind that cacao is more bitter than the chocolate we're familiar with and you'll need to adapt.

REISHI

ORIGIN — Mountainous forests of Asia.

LOOK — A woody mushroom that is round and flat with an orangey-red center. It grows on decomposing wild plum trees and sometimes on oaks as well.

BENEFITS — It's an immunomodulator, your immune system's strongest ally, and it works on your immunity in multiple ways, depending on its needs. It can strengthen a weak system just as it can moderate an over-reactive one—which can, for example, cause allergies and auto-immune diseases. It's also your best friend when you're struggling with fatigue, stress, anxiety, and insomnia. It can be taken as a supplement over one or more weeks, to prevent all sorts of diseases and boost your immune system.

BACKGROUND — The Japanese called it *reishi*, meaning "the king of plants." The Romans considered it to be the food of the gods, while the Egyptians believed it was a gift from Osiris, and the Chinese thought it the elixir of life.

USES — When seasons change, if you're under stress, or you're very tired. If you drink coffee, get into the habit of adding a little to your cup every morning.

WILD TIPS — Put 1 tsp in your favorite morning drink. Or even better, reishi plus chaga!

SPIRULINA

ORIGIN — Chad, Peru, India, Mexico, Madagascar.

LOOK — Spirulina looks like very fine green seaweed but it is actually a bacterium that has been around for over three billion years. It takes its name from its spiral shape.

BENEFITS — With extremely high levels of beta-carotene, iron, vitamin B12, vitamin E, proteins, minerals, and oligo-elements, it's the sport enthusiast's best friend (and kind to less sporty types, too). It is also very rich in antioxidants and contains the eight amino acids that are essential to our bodies. In short, this micro-alga boosts our immune system, purifies our blood, and increases strength and endurance.

BACKGROUND — Although often referred to as an alga, spirulina is more precisely a cynobacterium—a bacterium that produces its own energy by photosynthesis. This primitive organism, which has been around for 3.5 billion of our planet's 4.5 billion years, uses light to transform carbon dioxide into organic matter and generate oxygen. In his memoirs, Cortés, the fifteenth-century Spanish conquistador, recorded an Aztec practice that intrigued him, whereby the people walked by the lakes carrying tightly meshed nets to skim off a greenish mud that was spirulina. They would then dry it in the sun and use it to prepare cakes to eat.

USES — Sprinkle it on whatever you like, whenever you like, or take it in capsules as a supplement.

WILD TIPS — For a one-month course of treatment, stir 2–3 tsp into a glass of water or apple juice (organic, naturally) every morning. The vitamin C in the apple juice helps the body absorb the iron in spirulina.

my city guide: dubai

VEGGIE-FRIENDLY FOOD

Comptoir 102: This pioneer of healthy eating is not to be missed! Our ingredients are sourced from local organic farms and the menu changes according to the season and the harvest.
102 Beach Rd., Jumeirah 1
Tel. +971 (0)4 385 4555
www.comptoir102.com

Wild & the Moon: The first 100 percent vegan food concept in Dubai. Wild food, cold-pressed juices, nut mylks, and all the plant-based food choices you can dream of. And everything is homemade and organic. Several locations in Dubai, all with cool vibes: check Instagram to get a feel (@wildandthemoon).
3 locations
Tel. +971 800 9453
www.wildandthemoon.ae

Joga: Not vegan, but healthy and the food is delicious.
7 locations
Tel. +971 600 548 289
www.eatjoga.com

Freshii: Build your own salads, burritos, soups, bowls, and much more, all from the freshest ingredients. "Eat, energize" is their motto.
3 locations
Tel. +971 800 3737 444
www.freshiiuae.com

NKD Pizza (naked pizza): Their pizzas have no additives, no preservatives, no artificial flavors, and the tomato sauce is sugar-free. The gluten-free 10-grain crust with prebiotic is a must.
Shop 1, Kojak Building, Motor City
Tel. +971 (0)4 350 2017
www.nkdpizza.com

The Lime Tree Cafe: Cute little cafés that include a gluten-free bakery. Good for afternoon tea or a snack.
3 locations
Tel. +971 (0)4 325 6325
www.thelimetreecafe.com

Park House: Perfect after an exhilarating surf on one of Dubai's most beautiful beaches. The food is healthy, homemade, and the atmosphere is very chilled.
Kite Beach – 2 D St.
Tel. +971 (0)4 254 1565
www.kitebeach.ae/en/dine/park-house

Friends Avenue Cafe: Great for breakfast. The food is good—and "Instagrammable"—plus they serve fabulous coffee!
Fortune Executive – Ground Floor Cluster T, JLT
Tel. +971 (0)4 554 5813
www.friendsavenue.ae

Tania's Teahouse: Pink, girly, and sweet, this has been voted the 7th "Most Instagrammable Café in the World."
779A Jumeira St.
Tel. +971 (0)4 324 0021
www.taniasteahouse.com

Tashas: Healthy, fresh, and vibrant food served in chic surroundings with a welcoming vibe. Cool on weekends with the family.
The Galleria Al Wasi Retail Centre, Al Wasi St.
Tel. +971 (0)4 385 5500
www.tashascafe.com

Tom & Serg: An Australian-style café that is the perfect place to take the family or meet a group of friends. Happy atmosphere but a bit noisy.
15A St., Sheikh Zayed Rd.
Tel. +971 56 474 6812
www.tomandserg.com

Myocum: Go for the fresh food, the community spirit, and if you love good coffee. The must-try is the vegan brunch.
2 D St.
Tel. +971 54 530 5905
www.myocumdubai.com

Folia: A shady oasis surrounded by palm trees in the heart of the Four Seasons Resort, this is the perfect location to enjoy celebrity chef Matthew Kenney's plant-based menu.
Four Seasons Resort, Jumeirah Beach
Tel. +971 (0)4 270 7777
www.fourseasons.com/dubai

Urth Caffé: The first Urth café was opened in 1989, after the founders met a "passionate coffee farmer" from Peru and they made it their mission to serve health-conscious coffee. Don't miss out on their cappuccino and iced tea.
City Walk by Meraas
Tel. +971 (0)4 589 7413
www.urthcaffe.com

Arabian Tea House: As soon as you push open the door, you step back into Dubai's past. This quaint tea house in the historical neighborhood of Al Fahidi, once known as Al Bastakiya, serves authentic Emirati cuisine. It's the place to go if you want to try good local food.
Al Fahidi St.
Tel. +971 (0)4 353 5071
www.arabianteahouse.net

Avli by Tashas: A delightful Greek restaurant with authentic mezze, salads, and vegan specialties.
Unit C-01, 1st Floor, Gate Village Building 9, DIFC
Tel. +971 (0) 359 0008
www.avlibytashas.com

3 Fils: Dining is cool and casual in this modern Asian restaurant by Dubai's fishing port, which is run by renowned Singaporean chef Akmal Anuar. Not a lot of vegan options, but this still remains one of my favorite restaurants. A hidden gem.
Shop 02, Fishing Harbour, Jumeira 1
Tel. +971 (0)4 333. 4003
www.3fils.com

The Ripe Market: You'll find everything you're looking for at this market, from seasonal organic fruit and vegetables to freshly baked bread. Every Friday in Academy Park.
Sheikh Zayed Rd.
Tel. +971 (0)4 315 7000
ripeme.com/ripemarket

ORGANIC FARMS AND FARM SHOPS

Al Ain Bio Farm: The Emirates' largest private organic farm. Tasting tours can be booked online.
8th St., Abu Dhabi
Tel. + 971 (0)3 783 8422
www.emiratesbiofarm.com

Greenheart Organic Farm Shop: Freshly harvested, locally grown, and 100 percent organic.
The Light Commercial Tower, Arjan, Barsha South 2
Tel. +971 (0)4 361 7010
www.greenheartuae.com

LIFESTYLE

Comptoir 102: Hailed "Best Furniture Store" by *Harper's Bazaar* and "Best Healthy Restaurant" by What's On Awards, this concept store has also been named among the world's top nine destinations for its jewelry selection. The best independent fashion designers can also be found in this rock-chic boutique.
102 Beach Rd., Jumeirah 1
Tel. +971 (0)4 385 4555
www.comptoir102.com

O'De Rose: A boutique selling an eclectic mix of clothing, furniture, contemporary art, and accessories, as well as showcasing the work of local designers and artisans. If you're looking for souvenirs or gifts to take home, this is a great place to find them.
999 Al Wasl Rd.
Tel. +971 (0)4 348 7990
www.o-derose.com

Alserkal Avenue: A hub of creativity and definitely the coolest neighborhood in Dubai. With its many art galleries and trendy, atypical concept stores, Alserkal is unmissable. Drop in for lunch at Wild & the Moon and don't miss Gallery IVDE (Isabelle Van den Eynde): a contemporary space that displays work by Middle Eastern artists. I love it!
17th St.
Tel. +971 (0)4 333 3464
www.alserkalavenue.ae

That Hair Tho: My favorite hair and beauty salon. All the products they use are vegan and kind to the environment.
The Dome Tower, Cluster N, Shop NoB4 B5 B6
Tel. +971 (0)4 589 6679
www.thathairtho.me

SEVA: A yoga studio with a cute little vegan café—Goan vibes and good yoga classes.
27B St., Jumeirah 1, Jumeirah Beach Rd.
Tel. +971 56 534 2899
www.sevaexperience.com

ACTIVITIES

The Jam Jar: A community arts space with studios for DIY workshops, artists in residence, and exhibitions. Child-friendly.
Unit H74, Alserkal Avenue, Al Quoz 1
Tel. +971 (0)4 341 7303
www.thejamjardubai.com

Ras Al Khor Wildlife Sanctuary: An animal sanctuary and wetland reserve in the heart of Dubai. It attracts large flocks of amazing birds, including the famous pink flamingos.
Ras Al Khor Road, Ras Al Khor
Tel. +971 800 900 / (0)4 221 5555
www.rasalkhorwildlife.ae

Hatta: Not in Dubai city, but it is well worth the 90-minute drive to reach this restored, centuries-old village. Go hiking, bike riding or kayaking, while you admire the beautiful landscapes around you. You can also book a night in a luxury trailer.
www.visithatta.com

Old Dubai: A visit to the historical Al Fahidi district, with its many galleries, old souk, fishing port, and museum in the Al Fahidi Fort, is definitely worthwhile. Stop off in the lovely courtyard of the Hotel XVA in the Bastakiah district for a mint lemonade.
www.dubaiculture.gov.ae/en

Zabeel Park: Dubai's largest park and the perfect place for a breath of fresh air when you need to reconnect with nature. Take a picnic with the family or a group of friends— you could almost be in Central Park!
Zabeel Area, Near Al Jafiliya Metro Station
Tel. +971 (0)4 398 6888
www.dm.gov.ae

Dubai Water Canal: The best place for jogging early in the morning or at sunset, or just to feel the fresh breeze from the sea. There is a lovely view of the city, too. 2 miles (3.2 km) long, stretching from the Creek in Old Dubai to the Arabian Gulf.
www.visitdubai.com

Dubai Creek: Take a traditional boat and sail up the Dubai Creek, stopping off in the old souk to buy fresh spices.
www.visitdubai.com

Kite Beach: This white sand beach is my favorite. Go there for kitesurfing or a swim at sundown.
Tel. +971 (0)4 317 3999
www.kitebeach.ae

Nara: Take a trip into the desert (booked through Nara) to stay amid beautiful sand dunes. The eco-friendly **Sonara Camp** has a unique restaurant serving Arabic-inspired dishes and French cuisine, with live music and entertainment in the evenings. The private and exclusive **Nara Desert Escape** offers overnight stays in a traditional nomadic tent, with high-end dining and wellness activities such as yoga.
Tel. +971 (0)4 421 1356
www.nara.ae

Abu Dhabi: Visit the Louvre, have lunch at Wild & the Moon in the UAE's Cultural Foundation, and end your day at the Sheikh Zayed Grand Mosque, watching the sun set.

Yoga: The city has long offered numerous yoga classes, and there are plenty of places where you can experience a memorable early-morning sun salutation session. Jumeirah and Umm Suqueim beaches are my favorite spots.

Cycling in the desert: Dubai has 311 miles (500 km) of cycling tracks, just 20 minutes from the city center. The best times to go are at sunset or sunrise when the color of the light is magical and calm is guaranteed.

Running: Go for an early-morning run on the track at Jumeirah Beach next to La Mer, but avoid weekends when it gets very crowded.

my city guide: paris

VEGGIE-FRIENDLY FOOD

Septime La Cave: Natural wines and small dishes, each more delicious than the next. We love having an apéritif here before going to dinner at Clamato, its sister restaurant next door.
3, rue Basfroi, 75011
Tel. +33 (0)1 43 67 14 87
www.septime-lacave.fr/en

Faggio: Pizzas with very thin, crisp bases made from the finest ingredients and baked in a stone oven, plus natural wines. What could be better?
72, rue Marguerite de Rochechouart, 75009
Tel. +33 (0)1 40 37 44 02
faggio.fr

Aujourd'hui Demain: A Parisian temple of vegan dining, run by a Mexican chef who delights us with tacos and chili sin carne, as well as pancakes and tasty burgers. In the grocery store, you will find all your favorite vegan snacks, plant-based faux cheeses, and tofus of every color.
42, rue du Chemin Vert, 75011
Tel. +33 (0)9 81 65 20 01
www.aujourdhui-demain.com

Cheval d'Or: Dersou chef Taku Sekine's newest space, tucked away in Paris's 19th arrondissement. His French-Asian inspired menu will send you wild with delight.
21, rue de la Villette, 75019
Tel. +33 (0)9 54 12 21 77
www.chevaldorparis.com

Dreamin Man: The most charming little café run by the most charming Japanese couple. Drop by if you like really good coffee and homemade desserts.
140, rue Amelot, 75011
@dreaminman_paris

Ima Cantine: "Mama" in Hebrew (and "ami" spelled backwards!). This small vegetarian café serves dishes that remind you of the mouthwatering cuisine of chef Yotam Ottolenghi. The menu changes in the evening, switching to tapas mode.
39, quai de Valmy, 75010
Tel. +33 (0)1 40 36 41 37
www.imacantine.fr

Chiche: Israeli cuisine and natural wines. If you want to eat the best hummus in Paris, you'll find it here, along with every kind of shakshuka. And don't miss out on the meltingly soft eggplant—it's a pure delight!
29bis, rue du Château d'Eau, 75010
Tel. +33 (0)1 42 00 96 14
www.chicheparis.fr

Pastore: Opened by a group of Italian friends. Go to enjoy the original antipasti and fresh pasta with truffle, plus an excellent selection of natural wines.
26, rue Bergère, 75009
Tel. +33 (0)9 80 77 25 73
www.pastore.paris

Miznon: Highlights are the braised cauliflower (to die for), the mushroom pita (irresistible), and the ambience (cool), which evokes the streets of Tel Aviv.
22, rue des Ecouffes, 75004
Tel. +33 (0)1 42 74 83 58
@miznonparis

Abattoir Végétal: Our favorite vegan bistro for a plant-based brunch, serving homemade food that has as many flavors as it has colors. Everything is good and in season. Yum!
61, rue Ramey, 75018
Tel. +33 (0)1 42 57 60 62
www.abattoirvegetal.fr

Le Ruisseau: The best veggie burger is served here: tasty and full of fresh vegetables.
65, rue du Ruisseau, 75018
Tel. +33 (0)1 42 23 31 23
www.leruisseauburger.com

Grounded: A charming vegan coffee shop and plant-based eatery, where you can enjoy an oat milk dirty chai and salted turmeric scone. Everything is healthy, organic, in season, and delicious. Pop in for breakfast or brunch, but just don't miss out on this little restaurant with big ambitions.
101, rue de Charonne, 75011
Tel. +33 (0)6 84 44 63 53
@grounded_paris

Petit Pache: Run by the most delightful couple, this small wine bar is Paris's best kept secret. Feel free to question the *sommelier* as he knows everything about the provenance of his natural wines. The menu changes with the seasons and offers simple but well thought-out tapas.
7, rue Pache, 75011
Tel. +33 (0)1 77 15 08 19
www.hellopetitpache.com

Mokonuts: This coffee shop serves wonderful and inventive food, inspired by the diverse backgrounds (French, Lebanese, American, and Japanese) of the two geniuses who drive it.
5, rue Saint-Bernard, 75011
Tel. +33 (0)9 80 81 82 85
www.mokonuts.com

Echo: Californian-style deli and coffee shop. We are fans of the space, the atmosphere, and the superb American-inspired cuisine, created by a chef who is originally from Los Angeles.
95, rue d'Aboukir, 75002
Tel. +33 (0)1 40 26 53 21
www.echo-paris.com

Dersou: Taku Sekine's first restaurant and the one that bowled everyone over—without exception.
21, rue Saint-Nicolas, 75012
Tel. +33 (0)9 81 01 12 73
www.dersouparis.com/en

The Friendly Kitchen: Plant-based, organic, gluten-free food. Everything is homemade in this cosy space, which is a cross between a restaurant and a wine bar. Before calling in, we love to stroll around the beautiful streets of the 11th arrondissement.
8, rue Popincourt, 75011
Tel. +33 (0)1 43 57 33 42
www.the-friendly-kitchen.com

Le Jourdain: Ideal for a romantic evening or to meet friends. The cuisine is light and elegant, made from ingredients that are simple but exquisitely cooked. All the wines are natural.
101, rue des Couronnes, 75020
Tel. +33 (0)1 43 66 29 10
www.lejourdain.fr/en

Le Clown Bar: The cuisine focuses on short supply chains, sustainable farming, and wines with no added sulfites. We adore the lively atmosphere—it's one of my favorite places in Paris.
114, rue Amelot, 75011
Tel. +33 (0)1 43 55 87 35
www.clown-bar-paris-com

Tzeferakos: A small restaurant run by a Greek couple serving no-frills homestyle food. A one-way ticket to Greece that you won't regret.
24, rue Monge, 75005
Tel. +33 (0)1 46 34 76 27

Bistrot Hotaru: A bistro with an intimate atmosphere, where you'll believe you really are in Japan! Don't hesitate to go for the tasting menu, and don't forget to cast your eyes over the list of sakes. A Japanese restaurant with a fine reputation!
18, rue Rodier, 75009
Tel. +33 (0)1 48 78 33 74

Abri Soba: The soba (buckwheat) noodles are homemade, served firm and full of flavor, while the bento options are original and creative. But, in fact, everything is delicious!
10, rue Saulnier, 75009
Tel. +33 (0)1 45 23 51 68

Jah Jah By Le Tricycle: Choose from hot, cold, or raw bowl food, hotdogs, snacks, and desserts. Everything is 100 percent vegan and tasty!
11, rue des Petites Écuries, 75010
Tel. +33 (0)1 46 27 38 03

Peonies: Paris's first coffee and flower shop, serving great breakfasts, lunches, and vegetarian snacks.
81, rue du Faubourg Saint-Denis, 75010
www.peonies-paris.com

Café Berry: A simple menu of vegetarian, vegan, and gluten-free breakfast and lunch dishes that are colorful and beautiful.
10, rue Chapon, 75003
Tel. +33 (0)6 47 55 12 33
www.cafeberryparis.fr

Boulangerie Chambelland: The rice flour they use is milled at their own dedicated mill, so they can be certain any cross-contamination is avoided. If you love good gluten-free bread, this charming bakery is where you'll find it.
14, rue Ternaux, 75011
Tel. +33 (0)1 43 55 07 30
www.chambelland.com

Boulangerie Utopie: A cool bakery selling chocolate-coconut bread, black charcoal bread, delicious brioche, and divine pastries. Perfect for a gourmet breakfast or an indulgent snack.
20, rue Jean-Pierre Timbaud, 75011
Tel. +33 (0)9 82 50 74 48
@boulangerieutopie

Ten Belles Bread: All their doughs are made using natural yeast that produces a unique style of bread with a melting, generous crumb. As well as following bread-making methods that respect long fermentation times, they use only organic flour.
17–19, rue Breguet, 75011
Tel. +33 (0)1 47 00 08 19
www.tenbelles.com

Sain Boulangerie: Organic, kneaded by hand, natural yeast, ancient wheats—what more can I say, except go for it!
15, rue Marie et Louise, 75010
Tel. +33 (0)7 61 23 49 44
www.sain-boulangerie.com

Maison Loüno: Online store selling vegan, gluten-free, and sugar-free products, including black bread, granola, and adaptogen blends, that are all made in France. We love them!
www.maisonlouno.com

Marché des Enfants Rouges: The capital's oldest food market. We come to stock up on fresh produce and eat lunch on the go at the organic stall, the Italian grocery stall, or have a couscous or Japanese bento box.
39, rue de Bretagne, 75003

LIFESTYLE

Negozio Leggero: Our go-to store to stock up on all the essentials we need—from dried fruits and pulses to makeup, household items, and more—all loose and with no plastic packaging. Everything you need for zero-waste shopping!
37, rue Notre Dame de Nazareth, 75003
Tel. +33 (0)1 58 45 14 93
www.negozioleggero.it/en

Aime Skincare: The inside-out routine your skin has been waiting for. A happy gut makes for happy skin! A natural food supplement program by Mathilde Lacombe that will benefit your whole body.
3, rue du Pont aux Choux, 75003
Tel. +33 (0)6 42 34 56 31
www.aime.co/en

Oh My Cream!: Both a concept store dedicated to beauty and a temple of clean beauty brands. I adore the expert skin care tips unearthed by Juliette Levy.
9 locations in Paris
www.ohmycream.fr

Holidermie: Vegan cosmetics that are made in France and are super clean. Fashion stylist Mélanie Huynh has created this beautiful range.
21, rue de Marignan, 75008
Tel. +33 (0)1 71 18 14 30
en.holidermie.com

Patine: My absolute favorite fashion label. Patine challenges the fashion industry by creating quality, made-to-last, basic designs from recycled cotton. Ethical, practical, and beautiful.
18, cour des Petites Écuries, 75010
www.patine.fr

Sézane: A brand that is 100 percent committed to using ethnically sourced materials with a totally transparent manufacturing supply chain.
1, rue Saint-Fiacre, 75002
www.sezane.com

ACTIVITIES

La Cité Fertile: An inspirational place showing how the sustainable city deals with challenges not just through its eco-system, but also through programming and committed projects. It is a life-enhancing space open to all, welcoming residents, associations, companies, and solution providers.
14, avenue Edouard Vaillant, 93500 Pantin
Tel. +33 (0)1 48 43 04 60
www.citefertile.com

Dynamo Cycling Lafayette: Where you'll learn to love your bicycle again. The instructors are all cool and have their own individual style and playlist!
24, rue Chauchat, 75009
www.dynamo-cycling.com

TIHHY: Clotilde Chaumet's intensive Hip Hop Yoga! Our favorite yogi has added a touch of cardio for an intensified workout.
Book a class online at **www.tihhy.com**

Satnam Montmartre: Welcome to this yoga temple in the heart of Paris, where you can follow the city's best Kundalini courses with **Anne Bianchi** (**@satnam_montmartre** or visit **www.annebianchi.fr**). Take a class with **Lili Barbery-Coulon**, another of the high-priestesses of Kundalini (**@lilibarbery**), catch an Ashtanga class with **Klara Puski** (**@klarapuski**), or discover ballet pilates with **Jenn Becq** (**@joywithjenn**).

WILD & THE MOON

Cold
Pressed

Organic

Wild Food

Juice Bar

my city guide: new york

VEGGIE-FRIENDLY FOOD

Bareburger: High-quality burger chain with excellent plant-based options. Meat eaters, veggies, and those on a gluten-free diet can hang out here, where all the food is local, organic, and sustainable.
25 locations in NYC, NJ, and NY State
www.bareburger.com

Avant Garden: This tiny vegan restaurant in the East Village serves stylish vegan dishes accompanied by wines from around the globe. A good place for dinner.
130 East 7th St.
Tel. +1 646 -922-7948
www.avantgardennyc.com

The Butcher's Daughter: The three locations of this plant-based restaurant, café, and juice bar treat fruit and vegetables as a butcher would treat meat, chopping and carving them into healthy vegetarian dishes and pressing them into refreshing juices.
Nolita, West Village, and Williamsburg
www.thebutchersdaughter.com

Sweetgreen: Colorful salads and healthy homemade grain bowls using seasonal produce delivered fresh each morning.
Around 30 locations in Manhattan and Brooklyn
www.sweetgreen.com

Van Leeuwen Ice Cream: Classic ice creams, made with just a few fresh ingredients. They have many vegan options prepared using cashew milk, coconut milk, and other organic ingredients.
Numerous stores and trucks in NYC
www.vanleeuwenicecream.com

Altro Paradiso: Awarded two stars by the *New York Times*, this light, airy Italian space on Soho's west side serves some of the best pasta dishes in town.
234 Spring St.
Tel. +1 646-952-0828
www.altroparadiso.com

Cosme: A sleek restaurant in the Flatiron District serving contemporary Mexican cuisine, combined with seasonal ingredients from the Hudson Valley.
35 East 21st St.
Tel. +1 212-913-9659
www.cosmenyc.com

Roberta's: Famous for its wood oven baked pizzas topped with produce grown on a rooftop garden, this Bushwick institution seamlessly blends New York hipster-chic with authentic Italian. Be prepared to queue!
257 Moore St., Brooklyn
Tel. +1 718-417-1118
www.robertaspizza.com

Marlow & Sons: One of Williamsburg's first—and best—neighborhood restaurants and a "market-to-table" pioneer. The menu changes daily.
85 Broadway, Brooklyn
Tel. +1 718-384-1441
www.marlowandsons.com

Il Buco: Tucked away in a cobblestoned street in NoHo, this well-loved Mediterranean-Italian serves upscale dishes at well-worn communal tables, surrounded by kerosene lamps and copper pans. One of my favorites.
47 Bond St.
Tel. +1 212-533-1932
www.ilbuco.com

Blue Hill at Stone Barns: Chef Dan Barber sources his ingredients from the surrounding fields and local farms, showcasing the abundant produce of the Hudson Valley. There are no menus, guests are served a high-end tasting feast.
630 Bedford Rd, Tarrytown
Tel. +1 914-366-9600
www.bluehillfarm.com

Café Mogador: Serving exotically spiced Moroccan cuisine, this East Village eatery is great for brunch and is one of the city's best spots for people-watching.
101 St. Marks Place
Tel. +1 212-677-2226
www.cafemogador.com

Freemans: Hidden down an easily missed alley on the Lower East Side and with the atmosphere of a Colonial tavern. It's a great place to meet up with friends.
Freeman Alley
Tel. +1 212-420-0012
www.freemansrestaurant.com

Bar Pitti: It might be a Greenwich Village celebrity hangout, but Bar Pitti's classic Italian panini, pastas, and desserts make it the real deal.
268 6th Ave
Tel. +1 212-982-3300
www.barpitty.com

Black Seed Bagels: New York bagels poached "Montreal style" in honey water with seeds added before they are baked. The best bagels ever.
5 stores in Manhattan and 1 in Brooklyn
www.blackseedbagels.com

Taim Falafel: Taim means "tasty" in Hebrew, which tells you everything you need to know about this Israeli restaurant's falafels, pitas, and mezzes.
5 locations in Manhattan · www.taimfalafel.com

The Four Horsemen: James Murphy (frontman of LCD Soundsystem) serves New York's best selection of natural wines in his Brooklyn restaurant-wine bar.
295 Grand St., Brooklyn
Tel. +1 718-599-4900
www.fourhorsemenbk.com

Wythe Hotel Rooftop: Sip a cocktail and share small dishes in Lemon's rooftop bar with its spectacular view of the Manhattan skyline.
80 Wythe Ave, Williamsburg
Tel. +1 718-460-8000
www.wythehotel.com

abcV: Jean-Georges Vongerichten's restaurant inside the ABC furniture store serves plant-based dishes made with mostly organic and artisanal ingredients sourced from small and family farms. Creative and delicious!
38 East 19th St.
Tel. +1 212-475-5829
www.abchome.com

Little Choc Apothecary: This cosy little café is New York's first fully vegan creperie, serving both sweet and savory crepes.
141 Havemeyer St., Brooklyn
Tel. +1 718-963-0420
www.littlechoc.nyc

Di Fara Pizza: Fans queue for its thin-crust pizzas that have been made by its Italian owner for over 50 years and are regularly voted the best in New York.
2 locations in Brooklyn · www.difarapizzany.com

By Chloé: Plant-based salads, burgers, and cold-pressed juices are just a few of the grab-and-go treats at this vegan space.
5 locations in Manhattan · eatbychloe.com

Dirt Candy: This Lower East Side spot is New York's only restaurant serving nothing but vegetables. Stunning dishes such as spinach mille-feuille and pumpkin pad Thai look and taste unlike anything you've ever tried before.
86 Allen St.
Tel. +1 212-228-7732
www.dirtycandynyc.com

Double Zero: Matthew Kenney's vegan outlet specializes in plant-based pizzas, homemade nut-based cheeses, and a chocolate cake frosted with cashew milk ganache.
65 2nd Ave
Tel. +1 212-777-1608
www.matthewkenneycuisine.com

Nix: Close to Union Square, this is New York's only vegetarian restaurant with a Michelin star. Bright and buzzy, ingredients are seasonal and locally sourced.
72 University Place
Tel. +1 212-498-9393
www.nixny.com

Beyond Sushi: A vegan sushi chain at the forefront of the plant-based movement. They also serve innovative soups, salads, burgers, homemade pastas, and sharing plates.
6 locations in Manhattan
www.beyondsushi.com

Superiority Burger: An all-vegetarian fast-food outlet in the East Village. Their signature burger is made with Muenster cheese (vegan alternative available).
430 East 9th St.
Tel. +1 212-256-1192
www.superiorityburger.com

Orchard Grocer: An East Village all-vegan deli and food market that is a great place for healthy sandwiches, salads, and ice creams. Everything is palm oil-free and there are many gluten-free options.
78 Orchard St.
Tel. +1 646-757-9910
www.orchardgrocer.com

Smorgasburg: America's largest weekly open-air food market held on Saturdays on the Williamsburg waterfront and Sundays in Prospect Park. Great for a relaxed stroll.
www.smorgasburg.com

URBAN FARMS

Farm One: Manhattan's only indoor hydroponic farm in Tribeca, growing rare herbs, microgreens, and edible flowers. Guided tours available (book ahead).
77 Worth Street
Tel. +1 646-883-3276
www.farm.one

Brooklyn Grange: One of three New York farms that grow and distribute organic vegetables and herbs on rooftops. Tours available (book ahead).
63 Flushing Ave
Tel. +1 347-670-3660
www.brooklyngrangefarm.com

Gotham Greens: A vast greenhouse on the roof of Whole Foods Market in Brooklyn. Tours available (free, book online), with a tasting session at the end. The terrace is an ideal spot to have a beer.
214 3rd St., Brooklyn
Tel. +1 718-935-0600
www.gothamgreens.com

index

acknowledgments

Thanks to Ariane Geffard and Florent Massot for believing in me
and for bringing this project to fruition.

Thanks to my editor, Ryma Bouzid, for always being available
and cheerful, despite my (over-) packed diary.

Thanks to Daniele Gerkens and Océane Algaron
for their invaluable and enthusiastic participation.

Thanks to Greta Rybus for her discerning eye.

Thanks to my husband and cofounder of Wild & the Moon,
for putting up with our kitchen being overrun with seeds and superfoods
during the photo shoots, and without whom
the Wild & the Moon adventure would not have been possible.

Thanks to Mathilde Danglade, who I have been fortunate
to have by my side at Comptoir 102.

Thanks to Grégory Khellouf for having faith in this venture.

Thanks to Marie Le Troadec, my fantastic "partner in crime,"
for devoting so much time, energy, and good humor to this book,
which is, in (large) part, hers too. I'll miss you.

Thanks to my children, Thaïs, Joseph, and Vladimir, who awakened
in me the desire to fight for a cleaner planet.

Thanks to all those who have contributed from near or afar to make
Wild & the Moon such a virtuous and extraordinary adventure.

The Publisher wishes to thank

La Trésorerie
latresorerie.fr

Jars
jarsceramistes.com

Marion Graux
mariongraux.com

Merci
merci-merci.com

Datcha
datcha.paris

for the loan of their tableware
and fabrics for the photographs in this book.

WILD&THEMOON

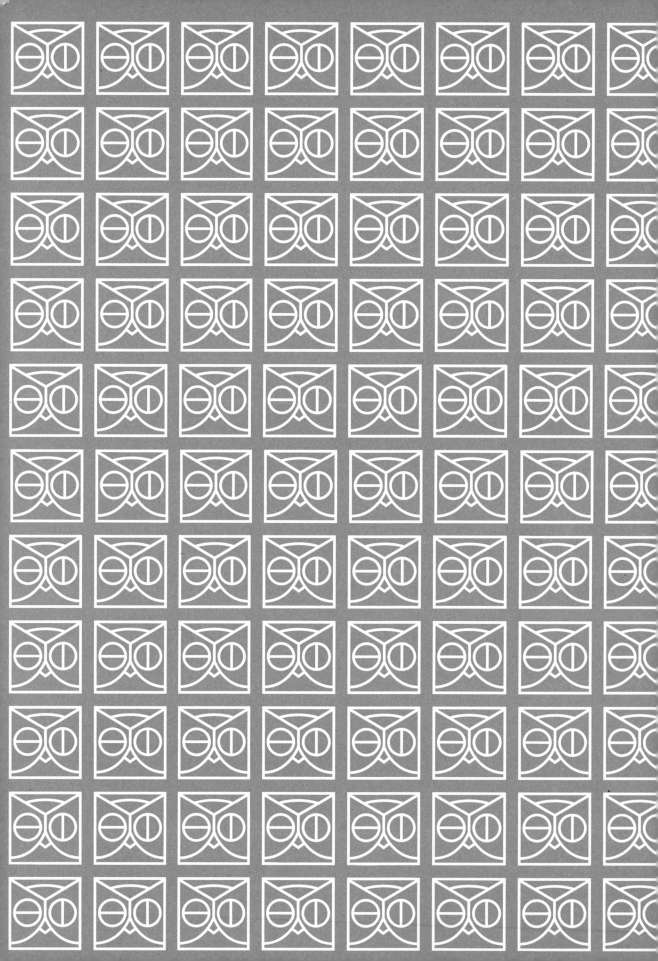